STARTING YOUR
CAREER AS A
CONSULTANT

STARTING YOUR
CAREER AS A
CONSULTANT

LETICIA GALLARES-JAPZON

ALLWORTH PRESS
NEW YORK

Allworth Press books may be purchased in bulk at special discounts for sales promotion, corporate gifts, fund-raising, or educational purposes. Special editions can also be created to specifications. For details, contact the Special Sales Department, Allworth Press, 307 West 36th Street, 11th Floor, New York, NY 10018 or info@skyhorsepublishing.com.

15 14 13 12 11   5 4 3 2 1

Published by Allworth Press, an imprint of Skyhorse Publishing, Inc.
307 West 36th Street, 11th Floor, New York, NY 10018.

Allworth Press® is a registered trademark of Skyhorse Publishing, Inc.®, a Delaware corporation.

www.allworth.com

Cover by Brian Peterson
Interior Design by Natalya Balnova

Library of Congress Cataloging-in-Publication Data

Gallares-Japzon, Leticia.   Starting your career as a consultant / Leticia Gallares-Japzon.   p. cm. Includes index. ISBN 978-1-62153-241-5 (alk. paper) 1. Consultants. 2. Consultants —Marketing. 3. Vocational guidance. I. Title. HD69.C6G35 2013 001 —dc23   2012040009

Printed in the United States of America

To my late brother, Angelo Abiera Gallares,
your presence is sorely missed.

To all my contributors, thank you for sharing your consulting
knowledge and experiences.

Contents

Preface

Starting Your Career as a Consultant is filled with samples, examples, checklists, practice exercises, mini case studies, personal anecdotes, war stories, common issues, suggested solutions, and key points. My intent is for you to use this book as a tool as you start your consulting career, and for you to continue looking at practices and trends to keep yourself up to date.

This book offers practical tips and step-by-step guidelines to help new consultants start a successful and profitable consulting career. Bite-sized, easy-to-read chapters cover setting your original idea, generating income, and much, much more to take you well on your way to success.

If you were to ask me: "Is the life of an independent consultant as great as it is cracked up to be?" I would answer yes—even greater. Once you are able to earn a basic living from this career, you will find that lifestyle and quality of life, not money, is the best reward, although a very good living can be had, too.

While you consider becoming self-employed as an independent consultant, you need to hear about the pros and cons as well as the how-to's. To meet this need is my purpose in writing this book. You may be allured by the flexible scheduling, the opportunity to choose for whom and where to work, and the potential for excellent compensation. Even more important is to know that you are bringing your unique expertise and skills to a set of issues and problems where you can "make a difference." Start-ups are more likely to be successful by focusing on a highly specific, very narrow specialty. Who are consultants? We are entrepreneurs in the knowledge field. We are people who believe that we are competent and can render a worthwhile service to others. Although consulting has become more popular over the years because of industry trends, it is not for everyone. You need a real purpose for going into consulting. If you intend to merely dabble in it without any clear goal, you will fail. As Thomas Carlyle once said, "The man without a purpose is like a ship without a rudder." This is especially true when starting a career.

What is consulting? It involves giving advice and providing innovative ideas and expert solutions for a fee. It is an expanding industry that offers incredible opportunities to those with the right background and skills.

Your first year of consulting is the most trying, particularly because you are just starting to establish your client base. It's a good idea to turn to your current employer before you quit your full-time job and negotiate with them whether they would like to be your first client on a contract basis. This way you would be working with people you already know and using familiar systems and procedures.

Success may not come immediately. It requires perseverance, determination, and a good measure of moral courage. More importantly, you must be able to stay focused and not get sidetracked. When things do not go according to plan (an eventuality you must prepare for), adjust your tactics and redouble your efforts—not only to solve your clients' business problems, but also to meet your own personal goals.

You see, consulting comes with responsibilities and dilemmas that you don't have to deal with as an employee. If you are unhappy with any aspects of your work or service, you are in charge of making the change. For instance, if the marketing technique you are using is not bringing you the kind of clients you want, try different tactics. Be flexible and try other techniques that will work best for you. Mix traditional and social media marketing approaches and use those that meet your needs. Whatever you come up with, the results will be yours to learn from and share with others.

You may find this hard to believe, but once you enter the consulting field, you will get to know yourself quickly. From the first week of your business, you will be continuously defining and redefining who you are, what you do, and what you have to offer clients. In the process, you will begin to call on strengths you never knew you had. Your opportunities for advancement are unlimited.

In consulting more than in any other business, honesty *is* the best policy. The reason is that you are the center of attention. Your clients are focusing on what you are offering. Be self-confident. Identify your positive points and use them.

Ask yourself seriously, "How do I implement my ideas? Does my service genuinely benefit clients? If so, in what way?" Tell clients what you can do but do not exaggerate your abilities. If you cannot deliver, sooner or later they will realize they are not getting what you promised. Moreover, exaggeration does not help your reputation one bit. Instead undersell—and exceed expectations!

Before you set up practice, ask yourself, "Do I have a product or service that can genuinely help clients? Can I deliver on my promises?" Answer these truthfully. Then decide if consulting is where you want to go. If it is, Welcome Aboard! The time is *now*.

As an independent consultant, you no longer have just one workplace with fixed working hours and workdays. You no longer have to attend endless meetings, some of which have nothing to do with your particular work and responsibilities. By taking charge of how you use your time, you can do more for a client company than you do now for your employer—and in much less time. And that time is of your own choosing. An immense opportunity exists for those in independent consulting. There is work that needs a consultant's experience and knowledge. There is money to be made. Above all, the excitement of new challenges and work environments keeps the work fresh and enjoyable.

Chapter One
Understanding the Consulting Business

The secrets of any business are to understand the customer's problems and to provide solutions to help them be profitable and feel good about the transaction.
—Francis G. Rodgers, former Vice President of Marketing at IBM

Understanding the consulting business is crucial for setting the right goals for yourself when you start this new career. Whether your plan to work as a consultant is short-term (less than five years) or long-term (more than five years), you have to continually assess how the consulting business is faring across the nation, industry by industry and by specialization. In addition, you want to keep up with current trends in the marketplace, both domestically and internationally.

CONSULTANT DEFINED
As I mentioned in the preface, a consultant is someone who has expertise in specific areas and offers unbiased opinions, advice, and innovative ideas and solutions to others for a fee. A consultant is not an employee but an independent contractor, usually self-employed, hired by companies to perform a short-term or long-term task, and paid on an hourly, daily, or project basis.

WHY PEOPLE GO INTO CONSULTING
Men and women choose careers as consultants for two main reasons: to generate more income and to be their own boss. In general, people who go into consulting may also:

- be frustrated with their current career because they see solutions to problems but are unable to effectively influence those who can implement those solutions;
- want a stimulating, dynamic, and growing career that satisfies their need for personal development;
- are unhappy with the lack of challenge, opportunity, or creativity in their existing job;
- are between jobs and seeking new opportunities and career;
- are at risk of being laid off and wish to establish themselves in a business that will let them continue to earn a living;
- have been laid off because of an economic downturn, government restructuring, or changing technology, which contribute to corporate downsizing, bankruptcy, mergers and acquisitions, reengineering, reorganizations, and so on;
- are retired but still have expertise and wisdom to offer;
- are retired but wish to continue earning an income because of recent financial setbacks, for example losing their money in stocks;
- are retired but still have the energy to contribute expertise to organizations who are seeking people with their skills;
- wish to supplement their current income by maximizing their managerial expertise and technical or academic skills;
- want to work from home and combine their family and work life.

The beauty of the consulting business is that you can start it with just one employee: YOU. You will have to work hard, but you can get a consulting operation up and running and make a very respectable start without involving a lot of other people in the project.

THINGS TO CONSIDER BEFORE GOING INTO CONSULTING

Ask yourself if you have what it takes before you start a career as a consultant:

PROFESSIONAL CONSIDERATIONS

- What special certifications and special licensing do I need? Depending on your area of expertise, you may need a special certification or a special license. For example, as an instructional designer and developer, you may be required to be certified in a specific courseware as a developer of computer-based training.

- Am I qualified as a consultant?

  Before you market yourself, make sure you have the qualifications and subject matter expertise necessary to get the job done. Some people assume that to qualify as a consultant you need to have many years of work experience. Depending on your expertise and industry, this might be true. But if you have very strong natural consulting skills or very specialized expertise, you can still consult others even if you can count the number of years of work experience on one hand.

  If you want to create websites for instance, make sure you are up-to-date on all the trends and changes in the computer industry. If you want to use a specific social media network to market your services, make sure that you are familiar with it and understand how to create your profile, how to market using your customized ads, and how to manage your information.

- Am I organized enough to become a consultant?

  Time management and organization ability are important. Ask yourself: Do I like to plan my day? Do I manage my time efficiently?

  Use this professional goals checklist to prioritize and create your action plan to achieve your short-term and long-term goals:

Table 1. Professional Goals Checklist

These goals will help you assess your decisions and choices. List each goal.	
Prioritize by listing your professional goals for the short term (one to five years):	List your professional goals for the long term (10 years or more):
1. Goal 1:	1. Goal 1:
2. Goal 2:	2. Goal 2:
3. Goal 3:	3. Goal 3:
4. Goal 4:	4. Goal 4:
5. Goal 5:	5. Goal 5:

Continues.

After you prioritize your goals, create an action plan for achieving each goal.

Action Plan	
1. Plan 1:	1. Plan 1:
2. Plan 2:	2. Plan 2:
3. Plan 3:	3. Plan 3:
4. Plan 4:	4. Plan 4:
5. Plan 5:	5. Plan 5:

FINANCIAL CONSIDERATIONS

- Am I financially ready?
  Finances weigh heavily on deciding when to become a consult-ant. You must be able to support yourself, your family, or any other dependents. Weigh your income versus your expenses; your earnings should be more than your expenses. If your expenses are more than what you earn, review all of your pro-jected income and expenses and make sure that you are in a favorable financial situation before you launch into full-time consulting. Assess your savings. You need at least six months' worth of living expenses to survive on your own.

Use this financial goals checklist to prioritize and create your action plan to achieve your short-term and long-term goals:

Table 2. Financial Goals Checklist

These goals will help you assess your decisions and choices. List each goal.	
Prioritize by listing your professional goals for the short term (one to five years):	List your professional goals for the long term (10 years or more):
1. Goal 1:	1. Goal 1:
2. Goal 2:	2. Goal 2:
3. Goal 3:	3. Goal 3:
4. Goal 4:	4. Goal 4:
5. Goal 5:	5. Goal 5:

Continues.

After you prioritize your goals, create an action plan for achieving each goal.

Action Plan	
1. Plan 1:	1. Plan 1:
2. Plan 2:	2. Plan 2:
3. Plan 3:	3. Plan 3:
4. Plan 4:	4. Plan 4:
5. Plan 5:	5. Plan 5:

PERSONAL CONSIDERATIONS

- Am I ready to quit my full-time job?
  Friends and family may ask why you would want to quit a good-paying job. Make sure you tell them why you want to make a change. It might be easier if you explain the reason to yourself first before you explain it to others.
  Am I ready to be my own boss?
  Being your own boss means managing yourself. Since you will be working for yourself, you have to find motivation to get your work done. This is where your organizational ability will count most.
- Am I ready to change my lifestyle?
  Working for yourself can mean a change in your lifestyle. You do not have the 9-to-5 schedule that you are used to when working as a full-time employee. Everything changes from the number of hours you work to where you work and how you work. For instance, if you have strict deadlines from a client, you may be working through the night while your family is sleeping, or you may be working twelve or more hours in a day, or you may be working weekends too. If you have a family that depends on you, ensure that they understand your schedule.
- What are my personal goals? Have I set short-term and long-term goals?
  Becoming a consultant requires serious planning and preparation. Make sure consulting fits into your personal goals, whatever those are (e.g., financial, professional). Remember that you can transition into consulting at your own pace. Do it in small

steps instead of going full force. Starting a career in consulting takes patience, perseverance, time, and effort.

- Do I like to network?
Networking is sharing information and services, as well as common interests, among individuals and groups. You can network casually or through direct means, both of which are useful. You may want to start networking with former colleagues who are now consultants and who know of your expertise.

A strong network is critical for becoming a successful consultant today. It is a marketing strategy that you can start immediately by building your network of contacts using either traditional or social media marketing approaches, or a combination of both. My friend Meryl, an independent consultant, advises to think things through seriously before you take the big leap and network with professionals who will help you. In her quest to work for herself, she used diverse networking approaches, one of which she recounts here:

> I thought long and hard before going into consulting. It took about a year for me to do research on my practice to establish a business and figure out how I was going to make enough income to transition. My husband doubted that I would be able to earn the salary I was used to. So, not only is it a wise idea to make a business plan, you must also consider how much savings, borrowing, or capital investment you are willing to risk to start working on your own. I rejoined a few professional organizations that I used to belong to, but had drifted away from in the years since work, marriage, a home, and children consumed my life. Many consultants attend professional organization functions that are offered monthly in almost every major city. It is a great way to network and find out what's new in your field, as well as to meet like-minded individuals who might know of some consulting work you can tap into. I was fortunate to meet a good friend and small business owner at one such professional

organization function who took me under his wing and assisted me in getting started. This meant taking a lot of consultants out to lunch, so be prepared to foot the bill in exchange for information.

Use this personal goals checklist to prioritize and create your action plan to achieve your short-term and long-term goals:

Table 3. Personal Goals Checklist

These goals will help you assess your decisions and choices. List each goal.	
Prioritize by listing your professional goals for the short term (one to five years):	List your professional goals for the long term (10 years or more):
1. Goal 1:	1. Goal 1:
2. Goal 2:	2. Goal 2:
3. Goal 3:	3. Goal 3:
4. Goal 4:	4. Goal 4:
5. Goal 5:	5. Goal 5:
After you prioritize your goals, create an action plan for achieving each goal.	
Action Plan	
1. Plan 1:	1. Plan 1:
2. Plan 2:	2. Plan 2:
3. Plan 3:	3. Plan 3:
4. Plan 4:	4. Plan 4:
5. Plan 5:	5. Plan 5:

TRANSITIONING INTO CONSULTING

Transitioning into consulting may be a big leap if you have worked for traditional organizations your entire career. Before you make a decision to change from a salaried employee to a consultant, ask yourself whether consulting is really for you because the change is not easy. Search within yourself and ask: Am I disciplined enough to be my own boss? Will my clients be willing to pay for my knowledge and services? How much should my clients pay for what I have to offer? Am I ready to quit my job? Can I survive without getting a steady paycheck? Do I have enough savings to get me started without giving me undue stress when bills and expenses continue to arrive? How will I obtain medical and dental insurance and will I be able to afford the coverage if I am not assured of a steady paycheck?

After you answer these questions, are you sure you are ready to make the transition? Is there a way to find out before you quit your full-time job? Is there a way to transition slowly or take it a step at a time or does it all happen at once? How do you make the first move to becoming a consultant?

Meryl had a smooth transition as she recalls here:

> The most valuable piece of advice I received for a smooth transition was to try to connect with the company I was already working for, which is easier said than done. Although I had the skills and the expertise to go "solo" and contract back (and they were in the business of hiring people like me on a contract basis), the transition was full of personal animosity and less-than-professional behavior. I did not truly know if I would be able to make it. Luckily, I was resourced out to another department that really valued my skills. Their appreciation was a godsend and I remained a consultant for that department for ten years. The key is *not* to burn any bridges because you never know if you will have to work with the same employer again at some point.

Indeed, many key factors come into play. A big one is money. You have to have the equivalent of at least six months' salary in the bank to sustain you while you are establishing a client base and waiting for your first consulting assignment. Even if you are aware of the many opportunities out there for consulting, you have to realize that you are not alone. Many others have embarked on this profession too. Competition is keen, so put your best foot forward when you sell your services.

With the current economy being at its worst, layoffs are rife throughout the industry and many high-quality managers and retirees are also looking for work. Most people looking for consulting assignments possess extensive experience and you are competing with them. If you have key contacts in major companies, you may have an upper hand, but still there are no guarantees.

Transitioning into consulting is a time-consuming task. You are in a balancing act between accepting an assignment offering low pay or waiting it out until you find one that pays more. You have to carefully assess your personal situation and see what will work best for you.

One of my independent-consultant friends, Frank, recounts his transition experience, which is very common:

> I spent four months looking. I tapped into all cash reserves and took out a few loans to sustain myself, pay heavy bills, and allow myself the means by which to career search. Just when I was about to run out of time, money, and energy (the culminating point), I was saved by a close friend who works as a program manager for the United States Government Science and Technology organization.
>
> While I am neither a scientist nor a high technology expert, I knew this opportunity would allow me to bring some basic organizational and management skills to the needs of a somewhat disorganized and sub-optimized organization. I would be subcontracted through a defense contracting company in support of the government. Although out of uniform, I would interact with senior military and civilian leaders and help them perform better—a far cry from the business world from whence I came, but closer to the world I knew. I still know many who are in positions of influence; and who trusted that I could bring personal experience and unique skills to meet their needs. *Voilà!*
>
> It appears that I will do more consulting work for this organization, and by building relationships and completing tasks, I was exposed to other organizations and opportunities. I now have alternative work options and positions of interest of relative importance. And they are in industries I can bring *my* background and personal skills to meeting their needs.
>
> As a management consultant, I try to be honest and support those who need help. I like the flexibility of being a management consultant, but there is an allure to accepting a regular position with a fine organization whose benefits and relative job security are solid. I wouldn't be able to find such position in Southern California, however. At least that is how it appears today. In the end, my fit within the industry, use of my set of skills, adequate compensation,

and ample time to spend with family and friends are the real considerations.

WHY COMPANIES NEED CONSULTANTS

Consultants are needed more so now than in the seventies, eighties, or nineties when companies kept significant numbers of salaried employees on their payrolls. The impact of downsizing, mergers and acquisitions, reengineering, and reorganizations is the major reason companies need consultants. Today, more and more companies that have reorganized their structure are outsourcing their service departments, such as human resources, accounting, and payroll as they find this to be cost-effective.

Consultants have become a necessity for companies that want to keep fixed costs down, yet still obtain the most current information. Consultants take on greater roles as projects become bigger, longer, and more complex, and as companies and individuals try to adapt to new technologies and constantly changing social and economic environments.

According to a recent survey conducted by Entrepreneur.com, there is increasing demand to hire consultants, because clients:

- want to simplify their day-to-day lives;
- have difficulty meeting deadlines;
- lack the expertise to do the job in-house (or themselves);
- are short on personnel;
- need an outsider who can look at a problem or situation objectively;
- want to capitalize on consultants' credibility to effect a change;
- want to avoid conflict in carrying out controversial or politically charged assignments, such as overseeing the reorganization of a company or merging of companies;
- want to hire people on a project basis to save on company benefits.

CONSULTING BUSINESSES THRIVING TODAY

If you are eligible for any type of 8(a) program (created by the Small Business Administration/SBA to help small disadvantaged business compete in the American economy and access the federal procurement market [whether you are], minority, women, or veteran-owned business), you ought to apply. It takes a while to complete the paperwork and pull out your Internal Revenue Service (IRS) statements, bank statements, and other needed documents, but it is very worthwhile. You are almost always required to carry a lot of insurance for your business and the cost could be high; this cost in itself should be part of your business expense. The federal government sets aside contracts for small business vendors, so check with your state and the federal government to see if you qualify.

My friend Meryl has worked with a number of small business owners who are operating under these federal government set-aside contracts, and this is another source of work for anyone who wants to go into consulting. Aside from federal government contract listings, you can also meet these people at professional organizations in your field, seminars, and other events. Meryl actively participates in American Society for Training and Development (ASTD) and International Society for Performance Improvement (ISPI) training events.

Another friend, Suzanne, said that consulting today is so much different than what it was when she started out in 1995. Of course, her focus is on Human Performance Technology (HPT) consulting, which has changed quite a bit in the past ten years; it might not be the same with other types of consulting. She has found that she has to be flexible, quickly adapt to change, and keep up to date in her field.

Many companies are in need of consultants who can provide expertise in specific fields. Currently, there are twenty consulting businesses that you can get into depending on your qualifications and subject matter expertise. Some examples include:

1. Accounting
   You can help a business with all of its financial needs; these could include bookkeeping.
2. Advertising
   This type of consultant is normally hired to develop a good strategic advertising campaign.
3. Auditing
   You can be hired to audit bills for small businesses or handle major auditing work for telecommunication companies.

4. Business

   If you have good business sense, you may do well as a business consultant. After computer consulting, people in this field are the most sought after.

5. Business writing

   Most businesspeople have trouble when it comes to writing a report, which may be an area you have expertise in if you have knowledge and experience in communications. This field is similar to the communications, editorial services, and writing services fields.

6. Career counseling

   With more and more people finding themselves victims of corporate downsizing, career consultants will always be in demand. You will guide your clients into a profession or job that will help them be both happy and productive as employees.

7. Communications

   You specialize in helping employees in both large and small businesses better communicate with each other, which ultimately makes the business more efficient and operate smoothly.

8. Computer consulting

   If you are computer-savvy and an expert in both hardware and software, your biggest problem will be not having enough hours in the day to meet your clients' demands.

9. Editorial services

   If you are an expert in the editorial field, you can help your clients produce newsletters, annual reports, and presentations.

10. Writing services

    Anything related to the written word will always be in demand. Technical writing and editing of proposals, for example, is one writing service that is currently in high demand.

TOP CONSULTING BUSINESSES

In searching resource books and the web, I found examples of the top consulting businesses in the greatest demand. This list in is not exhaustive. You can find much more information from other websites, books, and periodicals.

Table 12. Top Consulting Businesses

Specialization	Role of Consultants
1. Accounting	Provide bookkeeping and tax preparation services (solid career for a new consultant).
2. Advertising	Develop strategic ad campaigns.
3. Career Counseling	Help job seekers polish their résumés and prepare their job campaigns.
4. Computer Consulting	Design websites, develop blogs, install software and hardware, and create Internet marketing.
5. Education	Find scholarship money and advise students who are writing their college applications.
6. Executive Search (Headhunters)	Help companies create job positions, profile the labor market, and match highly skilled candidates with job vacancies.
7. Human Resources	Help with personnel issues like conflict resolution, violence in the workplace, sexual harassment awareness, and other people matters, not to mention those downsizing issues.
8. Insurance	Advise people about their insurance needs and find the best policies and best price (strong opportunity for a new consultant).
9. Management	Provide fresh ideas on how to manage a business better, especially in today's difficult economic times.
10. Public Relations	Meet with clients, find out how they are going to be perceived by the target audience, and design campaigns and media events.

To complement the hottest practices, you may also find the consulting trends in the twenty-first century helpful in determining where you are, how you can position yourself, and how you can update your skills to be successful:

- Technology planning, strategic services, and enterprise consulting are in high demand.
- Pursuit of specialized knowledge is rising rapidly. Companies are looking for consultants with very specific knowledge in areas like

logistics management, knowledge management, data warehousing, multimedia, client-server development, sales force automation, electronic commerce, brand management, and value management.

- Relationship building is soaring. This involves working with a company over many years to ensure continued monitoring, discussion, and implementation of innovative ideas.
- Including the client firm's management team as part of the consulting team. This facilitates implementation of ideas or getting buy-in into new ideas.
- More companies are looking for more business majors who have concrete analytical skills.
- Demand is increasing for consultants as a result of new global competition and sophisticated technological advances and innovations.
- Tremendous demand for skilled consultants who can work to link cable companies, web providers, online services, broadcast networks, wireless services, telephone companies, and publishers.

KEY POINTS

- Before you start your career as a consultant, take into account professional, financial, and personal goals. With those in mind, set your short and long-term goals and use checklists to prioritize them.
- Ask yourself: Am I ready to change my lifestyle? Do I like to network? Am I patient enough to spend a lot of time marketing my services? Am I ready to take the big leap to becoming a consultant? Am I ready to be my own boss?
- Review your qualifications and expertise, including your special certifications and licenses, and see where these would fit with your target clients.
- Know the client's business, the company culture, the problems to be solved, and the expertise you bring to the client's table. A company's culture is the way of life of a group of people— their behaviors, beliefs, values, and symbols. Find out the specific challenges that are facing the client's business, such as a need for "new management," or "prioritizing new opportunities."

- Reflect on your personal attributes to help determine whether your personality is really suited for consulting.
- Keep an open mind and understand that issues you encounter may vary.
- Clients will likely come to you with their most complex problems—and they will expect you to guide them to innovative and creative solutions.
- Build solid client relationships, draw on your strong analytical skills, and help to solve their problems, ultimately bringing satisfaction to you personally and value to the companies you represent.
- Review the consulting businesses that are thriving today and determine which one of these businesses you may be good at, can be involved in, or can practice.
- Review the top consulting businesses that are in great demand and determine where your expertise could best fit.

Chapter Two
Picking a Route That's Right for You

One day Alice came to a fork in the road and saw a Cheshire cat in a tree.
Alice: Would you tell me, please, which way I ought to walk from here?
Cat: That depends a good deal on where you want to get to.
Alice: I don't much care where —so long as I get somewhere.
Cat: Then it doesn't matter which way you walk.
—Lewis Carroll, *Alice's Adventures in Wonderland*

To be a consultant, you need to do an honest and thorough appraisal of your strengths and weaknesses. Only after you have identified your skills, talents, and attributes will you be able to determine your specialty areas and target market. Learn to package and sell your services and take advantage of opportunities. Having such awareness will enable you to project the self-confidence you need to run your practice and respond to questions that potential clients might ask. To know your strengths and weaknesses is a powerful part of your prescription for success.

ASSESSING YOURSELF
One of the important steps you want to take before you seriously delve into consulting is to take some self-assessment tests to evaluate your personal strengths and weaknesses. Many self-assessment tests are available, some of which are simple and easy to use. This book includes several personality tests you may want to complete. Start with *Exercise 1: Assessing Yourself.*

Exercise 1
Assessing Yourself

The following exercise will aid you in determining which direction you should take as a consultant. Complete it honestly and it will help you see if you are ready and competent enough to become a consultant. Go through the exercise periodically to keep your answers up to date.

Element	Your input
Summarize your résumé. Review each detail of your past experience, work positions, projects you have undertaken, education, credentials, and certifications obtained.	
List all of your areas of special interest, achievements, knowledge, and sources of personal satisfaction.	
List all of your skills and capabilities. Skills are acquired or developed abilities, such as researching and problem solving.	
List your talents. These are often unique or special, creative "gifts" or attributes. They can also be a combination of skills.	
List your inherent traits, such as being analytical, intuitive, sensitive, professional, reliable, self-confident, motivated, driven, responsive, or resourceful.	
Assess your psychological maturity, or constant readiness to relate to people and events.	
Describe your interpersonal skills, including the ability to gain the trust and respect of the client and to involve the client in the problem solving process.	
Outline your technical knowledge of the consulting business you want to get into.	
List all the skills and attributes you lack but which you believe are necessary to develop if you are to go into the consulting business.	
Write down how you propose to learn these skills and develop these attributes. Determine how long that will take. Set priorities.	

Continues.

18

State how your choices in the consulting business will be affected, if at all, if you believe you cannot develop the skills and attributes you lack.	
Write down how you believe you would run your consulting business.	
Think about how you intend to market your services, create a demand for your services, and make potential clients realize you exist.	

ASSESSING YOUR MARKETABLE SKILLS

Before you assess your marketable skills, ask yourself: Are your ideas and skills marketable? Your answer will help you decide whether you have what it takes to be an independent consultant. Check with people who are already consultants. Check with competitors. Test your ideas. Get some tips and information. See *Exercise 2: Evaluating Your Personal Attributes*.

Exercise 2
Evaluating Your Personal Attributes

This exercise helps you measure your personal attributes against those most commonly demonstrated by successful consultants. Using a 5-point scale, where 1 – *never* and 5 = *always*, check the column that most closely indicates how frequently you behave in potential consultative situations. Scoring instructions are given at the bottom of the chart.

Rating scale					Attributes
Never (1)	Seldom (2)	Occasionally (3)	Frequently (4)	Always (5)	Successful consultants:
					1 quickly build strong client relationships
					2 work effectively under extreme time pressure
					3 provide innovative solutions to difficult problems

Graph Continues.

Rating scale					Attributes
Never (1)	Seldom (2)	Occasionally (3)	Frequently (4)	Always (5)	Successful consultants:
					4 find ways to work through areas of conflict even when the client is wrong
					5 travel frequently even though it means sometimes being away from family for extended periods of time
					6 enjoy presenting in front of small and large audiences
					7 conduct thorough research and analysis when solving complex problems
					8 rapidly evaluate complex data sets to determine which information is most relevant
					9 help clients reach a diagnosis rather than simply offering their own version of the way things ought to be
					10 have the insight to know when a problem is not systemic or methodical

(# x 1)   (# x 2)   (# x 3)   (# x 4)   (# x 5)

_____ + _____ + _____ + _____ + _____ =
_____ (Overall score)

Never Seldom   Occasionally   Frequently Always

Scoring: Tally check marks by column, then multiply the total by the number assigned to that category. (For example, five responses of "occasionally" x 3 give you a score of fifteen for that category). Adding the total across categories gives your overall score. Scoring between forty and fifty indicates you are already using many consulting skills and have a high potential for success in the profession. Falling between thirty and forty suggests you possess a number of the desired attributes, but could benefit greatly from sharpening your skills. Scores below thirty may indicate that you might want to think about whether consulting is the right path for you.

WHAT ARE YOU REALLY GOOD AT?

Who are you? What can you offer to others? Think about your decision-making strengths: What are they? Can you meet the tasks that your prospective clients will set out for you to do? Are you confident in relying on your own judgment and making decisions? Your answers will help you decide what work to pursue. How have you prepared yourself to meet your life goals through work? Stay in touch with the primary tool of your trade: yourself. See *Exercise 3: Test Your Decision-Making Strengths.*

Exercise 3
Test Your Decision-Making Strengths

In this exercise, you are assessing your decision-making in new or unfamiliar situations, the results you can be counted on to deliver for a period of time, and your ability to turn weaknesses into strengths. As a potential consultant, you are looking to see which of the following thinking styles most reflect your own: the Knower, the Conciliator, the Conceptor, or the Deliberator.

Below are descriptions and examples of each thinking style you need to understand before you begin this exercise. Remember that you can have one or more of these decision-making skills, whether you are a client or a consultant.

Decision-Making Skills			Put a check mark next to the style that best represents your decision-making strength. In the last column, list reasons why you think …	
Style	Description	Example	(√)	Reasons
The Knower	Brings clarity and focus to a decision	Making logical unemotional decisions or reaching clear conclusions quickly		
The Conciliator	Gets people involved and excited about a plan	Keeping communications open with others		
The Conceptor	Sees rapid and broad (left-brain/right brain) "overview" of decisions in new situations; is inventive; reformulates basic assumption; has a clear vision of future possibilities by combining logic and imagination.	Focusing on one thing in particular, such as business.		
The Deliberator	Takes longer to assess situations to reach a decision; analyzes, plans, and delivers the plan; overall, is steady in his work.	Demonstrating mastery of your craft, your in-depth experience in entrepreneurship, and your wide range of interests.		

Exercise 3a
Summary of Decision-Making Strengths

When you provide a consulting service, you need to focus on the problems that your client hires you to resolve. You should be able to conceptualize and thoroughly use your decision-making skills. Whether you are a client or a consultant, you can benefit from having any or all of these decision-making skills.

The Knower	The Conceptor
Patience with a client's more thoughtful decision-making is continually tested.	Has a high potential for conflict if both client and consultant are strong, dominant types. Agreement can be reached on goals.
Can be a win-lose situation if both client and consultant stick too closely to their own decisions, with no compromises or flexibility.	Wants openness on a daily basis.
The Conciliator	**The Deliberator**
Resolves conflict and uses communication tools effectively. Is creative.	Typically delays decisions. Has all the relevant facts and reflects vividly on those facts.

WHAT AREN'T YOU SO GOOD AT?

Look your strengths and weaknesses in the eye. When clients are interested, you should be able to tell them who you are, what you can do well, and what you are not so good at. A part of how you see yourself is how you think others see you. More useful, however, is a match between how you see yourself and how others *actually* see you. Ask yourself and ask your clients how they perceive you: How do they think you see yourself? Since you tell clients how you see them and their work, turning that question around seems reasonable.

Your livelihood as a consultant depends on accurate readings of your clients' perceptions of you; you need to know how you are coming across. Is your impact on them positive or negative? List your weaknesses and the gaps in your competencies and turn them into strengths.

Be confident, but don't overdo it because overconfidence may backfire. Generally, if you are overconfident about your strengths, you:

- discuss the project in such detail with your clients that you lose sight of what your proposal states has to be accomplished;
- are so enamored with your ideas that you do not listen to your clients' concerns or needs.

THE MYERS-BRIGGS PERSONALITY INVENTORY—PERSPECTIVES

The Myers-Briggs Personality Inventory is a personality test used by many organizations and schools. In the business world, organizations use it to make hiring decisions and identify leadership potential. In schools, Myers-Briggs is used in career counseling to help guide students into appropriate fields that match their personality type.

It can help guide you when you are looking to identify and understand your specific personality type. If you are seriously considering becoming a consultant, think about the underlying features of the work you really want to do.

These features should serve to:

1. provide an opportunity for you to use your special abilities;
2. permit you to be creative and original;
3. give you an opportunity to be of service to others.

If you want to take the Myers-Briggs Personality Inventory, contact a certified counselor, career counselor, psychologist, or other qualified professional in your area. If you are unable to find a referral through someone you trust, write to the National Board for Certified Counselors in Greensboro, North Carolina.

Before joining Xerox Corporation, I worked at The World Bank in various capacities. In the late eighties, I went back to school and took night classes. Here is my personal experience with the Myers-Briggs Personality Inventory as an employee in a training organization and as a graduate student.

When I worked for the World Bank in professional/technical training, each of us in the group was asked to take the Myers-Briggs Personality Inventory to find out if we could successfully team up with others who had opposite personalities. I found the results an eye-opener. I knew that I was an ISFJ (Introverted-Sensing-Feeling-Judgmental).

A year or so later, when I was a graduate student at George Washington University majoring in instructional design and development, one of our professors required that we take the Myers-Briggs Personality Inventory. Based on our individual results, he decided to pair me with someone who was exactly opposite from my personality. Mark (a colleague from the World Bank who was working in management training) and I worked well together. His approach was to jump from one instructional design step to another, whereas I preferred to follow the design sequentially. The project was successful because we complemented each other's skills. We received the highest score for our training program and I learned that partnering with opposite personalities can work. Both people just need to be flexible and open-minded about each other's ideas and opinions.

This experience is relevant to your own role as a consultant. You have to be flexible and open-minded when you work with your clients —collaborate; adapt and adjust; give and take.

Others' experiences with the Myers-Briggs have equal merit. Take the view of Frank that considers this test as a more revealing and more interesting personality test than the thinking style strengths. He says, for his money, this is an excellent and enjoyable personality profile.

Frank adds:

> In a positive manner, Myers-Briggs identifies your personality type as well as those of others with whom you interact. Each time you take the inventory, you reveal more of your preferences.

> There are all sorts of tests and profiles out there for you to "consider." Each is unique and "may" provide some utility to you as you select a course of action in a life or job change.

> I suggest that you be selective in taking these, and ensure that you have the benefit of an expert who can help interpret the results and put them in perspective. You must then determine how important the results are to your decision-making process.

Suzanne says:

It is important to use as much fact-based evidence as possible to make decisions. I would tend to be cautious when applying "popular" tools, surveys, inventories, and others, as the basis for critical life decisions. Myers-Briggs could provide a little insight but it shouldn't be the sole factor for deciding whether or not to be a consultant.

MENSA'S SELF-SCORING PERSONALITY TESTS

Mensa's self-scoring personality tests look at a few distinct personality types. These personality types are introversion/extroversion, emotional stability, creativity, and strong-mindedness.

Ideally, as a consultant, you will find it valuable to have the following characteristics:

1. Extroversion: outward-looking, friendly, uninhibited.
2. Emotional stability: steady, balanced, calm, unflappable, and imperturbable.
3. Creativity: leaning toward variety naturally, even if you are not instructed.
4. Strong-mindedness: a right attitude toward life and other people. It could be called the competitive versus cooperative approach or the self-centered versus caring attitude.

If you are interested in Mensa's personality tests, you can easily buy a workbook at most bookstores. For further information, write to:

American Mensa, Ltd.
1229 Corporate Drive West
Arlington, TX 76006-6103
Email: NationalOffice@americanmensa.org
Phone: (817) 607-0060
Fax: (817) 649-5232

THE CONSULTANT LIFESTYLE

It is either feast or famine in this business. The reality is going to always be different than you planned. Either you won't have enough work to keep you busy, or you will be working three jobs all at once. How much work you choose to take on will depend on how much you want to grow and expand your business—if you want to, and if you enjoy doing the work yourself, or even want to use others to do the work. In any case, you will be busy.

Finding your first assignment will not be easy. Start by seeking out former colleagues or acquaintances who are already working as consultants. Get their advice because going into consulting without any clients is not easy.

A lot of work is involved, from the networking to the marketing. You not only have to do all the work but you have to find the clients. Once you find them, keep them, and work on things that clients require from you. Other tasks that you would have to do are to keep the books and finances, to plan your travel, to participate in meetings, and so on. You should already be used to these tasks, and they are an exciting part of being a consultant. You can enjoy being your own boss and work for clients directly. Consultants are usually respected for their expertise so you only perform the tasks that are required based on your contract specifications.

Meryl has been successful working with different clients for the last ten years:

> My time is my own. If I want to work weekends, I do. If I have a stringent deadline, I am able to get work done because I control my own hours. If I want to spend time with my family and am not super busy, I can attend my daughter's school function during the day. Time and organizational skills are important because I have to be able to plan ahead based on my work schedule. I usually plan things two to three weeks in advance and accept client work on a first-come, first-serve basis, especially when I have several clients signed up. When a client signs a formal contract, it is binding and my work starts. I always ensure that my clients sign my contracts; without a signature, requirements are subject to change.

> Working as a consultant gives me joy, flexibility, and satisfaction with life. I am able to work from home and enjoy combining work with my personal life. Sometimes, I get

to go to the gym, the supermarket, cook, read, travel, and do other fun things with family and friends. I cherish this blended lifestyle.

One piece of advice, however, is to plan for downtimes. If you plan to pay quarterly taxes, save about 30 percent of your paychecks for the IRS. I was not always successful in doing this and it can add stress to your life come tax time.

TYPE OF PERSONALITY THAT RESPONDS WELL TO CONSULTANT LIFESTYLE

It is difficult to typecast people since there are many consultants for so many different areas of expertise. People that have the following personalities respond well to the consultant lifestyle:

CONFIDENT
Confidence comes from years of practical application in many different situations, working with clients, being comfortable with all levels of management, having knowledge and keeping up with technology, the industry, and contracting.

Convince yourself and your clients that you can do the job. This doesn't mean that you have to know it all, but you have to be confident that you can find the best solutions to your clients' problems and apply your knowledge and experience successfully.

PROBLEM SOLVER
Be passionate about solving problems because this is what you will be doing all day. To problem-solve, you have to be able to brainstorm possible solutions, isolate the implications of each solution, narrow your solutions, and choose the best one for the problem.

MOTIVATED
Keep yourself on task, especially if you work from your home office or in a remote location. Make a conscious decision to get up the same time each morning like you are actually going to the office. Set goals, actively seek out mentors like a consultant friend who might have been in the consulting business for a while and perhaps you can bounce

off your ideas, ask for their advice, share your thoughts, and ask for feedback.

OBSESSIVE
Many of the problems you may encounter may need a lot of your attention for long periods of time, meaning you need to be able to process a problem in the back of your mind when you are not giving it full attention and taking care of other tasks.

LATERAL THINKER
Lateral thinking is solving problems through an indirect or creative approach using reasoning that is not immediately obvious. See beyond the task at hand and question the assumptions that lead to a problem. This will help you predict problems and find opportunities to provide solutions.

PERSONABLE
Have a great personality, be a real people person. You will be involved in more than one company culture and, as a consultant, you will be viewed as an outsider in the beginning.

FLEXIBLE
Accommodate the priorities of multiple clients, as well as be flexible about managing your time and money. For example, your monthly income will be up and down as projects come and go; and sometimes, you might have trouble getting your fee on time.

ASSERTIVE
Although you try to be flexible on most things, stand your ground on things that matter, like getting paid on time. Be willing to lose a client to defend your position in a case like this.

HONEST
Always speak the truth. Your integrity is your most valuable asset; once you lose it, it is difficult to get it back.

REALISTIC
This trait may seem to conflict with the nine other traits above, but you have to realize that you cannot work 24/7. Give yourself a life outside

of consulting and be able to admit when you make a mistake or need someone's help.

KEY POINTS

- Compare what you are good at and not so good at—your strengths and weaknesses.
- Focus on your weaknesses and determine how you can transform them into strengths.
- Use self-assessment inventories or tests to assess yourself and your marketable skills.
- Use an appropriate personality test to determine your personality type, thereby helping you determine whether becoming a consultant is a good fit for you. Bear in mind that Myers-Briggs is just a tool to provide you with insight. Try fact-based tests to help you make a clear decision whether consulting is right for you.
- Take baby steps before you transition into full-time consulting.
- Determine whether you have the personality traits necessary to be an effective consultant.

Chapter Three
Setting Up Your Business

It used to be that a guy went into the Army when everything else failed; now he goes into the consulting business.
—Sportscaster Blackie Sherrod

Every contract you enter into as an independent consultant will have different mechanics and expense procedures. If you are contracted directly by the client and submit expense reports like other employees, the turnaround time for reimbursement may take only a week or two (within the payment cycle of credit cards you may be using). If you are subcontracted through a prime vendor (sometimes known as a job shop) and submit your billing and expense reports to them, they in turn must bill the client. This process can take significantly longer to complete. You could get paid thirty or forty-five days or longer from the time you submit your invoice.

Here is Frank's experience with the billing process, which can be a big disadvantage for you, unless you have available cash for your operations while you are waiting to get paid:

> As a subcontractor for the federal government, my prime vendor provides extensive support to the client and has an established billing procedure that is mature and efficient. Nonetheless, it frequently takes my vendor forty-five days to get payment from the federal government and another

few weeks for me to get a check from the vendor. This clearly puts me out of pocket for paying heavy expenses, which I acquire in travel, lodging, meals, and salary for work performed. I am always getting paid forty-five to sixty days behind.

This is not unworkable once the work rhythm stabilizes and the expense reporting and payment process becomes a matter of routine. However, the first several months of work may be a dry period for you, as the process of billing, liquidation of claims, and check-cutting occurs. Be prepared. Know upfront how your arrangement will affect your costs and ability to pay mounting bills.

My own experience working for quasi-government agencies has been better than Frank's. It has usually taken 30 or fewer days to receive payment for my invoices.

GETTING INTO GEAR

After you have assessed your skills, attributes, and abilities and determined your area of interest and expertise, you can move on to administrative basics. This is the fun part because it involves successfully marketing your consulting business.

Before setting up business and opening your doors to the public, consider your fee structure, marketing plan, and business plan. Your business plan includes your cash flow projections to determine how much money you need to generate to cover your overhead expenses.

SETTING UP YOUR BUSINESS

1. Timing
   Many of you do not entertain thoughts of consulting until the stark realization occurs that you are job hunting along with tens of thousands of others. These others have industry experience, accessibility to corporate managers, and résumés that are as good or better than yours. As the clock ticks on, you simply need to work, bring money in, and etch out a lucrative and satisfying career path. To be sure, taking the step to become an independent consultant is a "leap of faith." Taking

that leap at the point when you are financially challenged can be frightening.

You know you need to build business. Not just for now, but for the future. This takes time and money. It takes time once you have begun work to get paid. As stated earlier, payment of fees and reimbursement for expenses can take months. If you accept the challenge of becoming a consultant at a time when your bills are mounting and you have had no income (as many of us do), the time it takes to see cash flowing in must be fully understood.

2. Start-up costs and monthly expenses

Start-up costs depend on your choices and situation. Use a start-up expense checklist to estimate the initial costs of your business and to determine whether and how these costs can be met with your projected cash flow. Keep records of your estimated and actual overhead expenses and costs during the start-up and first year of operation, once you've made the decision to continue consulting.

Every business faces one-time start-up costs plus monthly expenses. You must systematically plan for these expenses, although it is impossible at this point to put them in actual dollar amounts. You can only estimate, using the sample checklist on the next page. Costs depend on many factors: your location, your type of consulting business, your plans, etc.

Use this start-up checklist as a guide to the kind of expenses typically incurred by new consultants. Fill in the amounts you expect to pay during your first month of business and an average for each succeeding month. Of course, some of these expenses may not be necessary for *you*, depending on how you set up your business.

When you look at your Sample Start-up Monthly Expense Checklist you see that you will be faced with numerous expenses at first. The big-ticket items are furniture and equipment. See chapters 4 and 11 for discussions of home office furniture and equipment.

Table 4. Sample Start-up Monthly Expense Checklist

Instructions: This checklist is only a guide. Your expenses will vary depending on whether you are setting up your home office or renting an office space. Go through this list and fill in dollar amounts tailored to your particular situation.

Setting Up Your Home Office

Expenses	1st month	Avg. month
Rent (if needed)	_____	_____
Office equipment (e.g., computer, fax machine)	_____	_____
Office preparation & maintenance	_____	_____
Utilities (e.g., electricity)	_____	_____
Telephone (e.g., set up toll-free number)	_____	_____
Postage, mailing, and shipping (e.g., UPS, FedEx)	_____	_____
Furniture and fixtures	_____	_____
Paper supplies, stationery	_____	_____
Internet access	_____	_____
Website design & maintenance	_____	_____
Insurance (e.g., professional liability)	_____	_____
Reproduction (e.g., photocopying machine)	_____	_____
Answering machine or services	_____	_____
Subcontracted services (e.g., billing)	_____	_____
Attorney's fees	_____	_____
Accountant's or financial advisor's fees	_____	_____
Business licenses and permits (continuing)	_____	_____
Promotional materials (e.g., brochure)	_____	_____
Travel (out of town)	_____	_____
Training (conference fees)	_____	_____
Business meetings and entertainment	_____	_____
Professional dues	_____	_____
Books & subscriptions	_____	_____
Logo design	_____	_____
Writing & editing of materials	_____	_____
Client gifts	_____	_____
Charitable contributions	_____	_____
Salaries (if you plan to hire employees)	_____	_____
Retirement / pensions	_____	_____
Miscellaneous (contingencies)	_____	_____
TOTAL EXPENSES	1st mo.	Avg. mo.

3. Time Management.

Time is a precious commodity. While this appears evident, time is particularly important to you, as a consultant since you charge for your services by the hour or by the day. Your time has to be involved not only in doing the tasks of the job, but also in managing the business (administrative, financial, logistics, legal, and so on). Developing a new business and expanding your current business are important and time-consuming matters facing you continually.

SELECTING YOUR NAME

Consider two factors when selecting a name for yourself and your business:

1. Your own name.

Many consultants do business under their own name. For example, my former business partner, Mary, and I worked as independent consultants as instructional systems designers and developers. We decided to select the first letters of our last names and conveniently called our collaboration JAE Design. (JApzon and English).

When you decide to use your own name as an independent consultant(s), both your business card and letterhead stationery should show the same name and telephone number (with area code) and a brief description that could read, for example, "Instructional Systems Design."

2. Fictitious name.

If you are operating your own consulting business as a sole proprietor under a name other than your own, you are required in most states to register your fictitious name. Using a fictitious name is called "Doing Business As" or DBA. You cannot apply for a DBA if you are a corporation. The procedures vary from area to area. Generally, the procedure involves filling out forms disclosing the name of the person or persons behind the name. You need to choose a name that is not already in use. You can find more information on registering for a DBA on the U.S. Small Business Administration website: www.sba.gov/content/ register-your-fictitious-or-doing-business-dba-name/.

WORKING SOLO

If you decide to work alone, you are in a sole proprietorship, which means you own the business by yourself. This is the easiest, least expensive, and least regulated business legal structure. You can run the business by yourself or you can hire some employees. As an independent consultant, you are most likely to work by yourself and subcontract any work overflows that you have no time to finish by yourself. All freelancers are considered "sole proprietors," which is another way of saying "self-employed." As a freelancer, my expertise is instructional design and development. I use a market-based method to charge my fee per hour. A market-based method is calculated by using a rate set by other consultants with similar skills. In my last project in 2011, I charged $100/hour for conducting research and designing and developing instructional lessons and materials. My fee per hour ranges from $80 (low), $100 (median), $125 (high), to very high ($150).

Table 5. Sole Proprietorship

Advantages	Disadvantages
Ease of formation. Fewer legal restrictions associated with forming a sole proprietorship.	**Unlimited personal liability.** You are responsible for the full amount of business debt, which may exceed your investment. Your liability extends to all assets, such as your home and vehicle.
Least expensive to establish. Costs vary according to the city in which the business is formed, but usually include a license fee and may include a business tax. You can obtain this information by calling the business license bureau of your city government. If you live in an unincorporated area, contact your county offices. You can find more information on the U.S. Small Business Administration website.	**Limited growth potential.** The future of the company is dependent upon your capabilities in terms of knowledge, drive, and financial potential. Also consider a simple process capability—there are only so many hours in a day.

Continues.

Fewer records are needed because of fewer regulations. While regulations vary by state, as a sole proprietor you can generally be established by registering your company's name and obtaining a business license.	**Heavy responsibility.** You are the only person who can evaluate office equipment and make the buying decisions. You have the ultimate responsibility for the purchase of supplies, equipment, advertising, and insurance. You also handle employees, marketing, bill paying, and customer relations.
Taxed as an individual. As the sole owner, your business's profit and loss are recorded on Federal Tax Form 1040, Schedule C, and the bottom line amount is transferred to your personal tax form. You file Schedule SE, which is your contribution to Social Security.	**Death, illness, or injury can endanger the business.** As the sole owner, your business ceases to exist as a legal entity upon your death.
Total control. You own and operate your business as a sole owner. You make all the decisions and you have total responsibility and control of the business.	

Source: Pinson, Linda, and Jinnett, Jerry. *Steps to Small Business Start-up*. Chicago: Kaplan Publishing, 2006 (pp. 35–47).

The sole proprietorship is best suited for a single-owner business for which taxes or product liability are not a concern.

The sole proprietorship is the most common form of business and comprises 70 percent of all American business entities. Many who are just starting a business choose this form because it is the easiest to operate until it becomes practical to enter into a partnership or to incorporate.

WORKING WITH PARTNERS

A partnership is two or more people working to carry on as co-owners of a business for profit. Although not required by law, you may have to submit written articles of partnership, which define each partner's role and contribution to the business (financial, managerial, and others). All articles should be filed with the Secretary of State.

Table 6. Partnership

Advantages	Disadvantages
Ease of formation. Allows two or more people to work together and bring different skills and resources to the business.	**Personal liability.** Partners are personally responsible for paying all of the debts and obligations of the partnership.
Easy to establish. The actual registration of a partnership is not expensive or complicated.	**Liability** for bad business decisions or negligence. Each partner is personally responsible for the actions of the other partners. If one partner makes a bad business decision or acts negligently, resulting in the partnership owing a debt, all partners are personally responsible for paying the debt.
Taxation. If the partnership suffers a loss but the partners have other employment income, their portion of the loss can be used to reduce their taxable income, thereby lowering each partner's personal income tax.	**Single legal entity.** Because a partnership is based on the individual partners and is not a separate legal entity, if one of the partners dies, the partnership ends. The remaining partners have to re-establish the partnership.

WORKING WITH A CORPORATION

Working with several people is called a corporation; this arrangement is more complex than a sole proprietorship. A corporation is a distinct legal entity, separate from the individuals who own it. The authority of the state government forms it, with approval from the Secretary of State. If business is conducted in more than one state, you must comply with the federal laws regarding interstate commerce. Federal and state laws may vary considerably.

Table 7. Corporation

Advantages	Disadvantages
Ownership. Ownership is readily transferable. The corporation does not cease to exist with the death of an owner.	**Extensive government regulation.** Corporations are complex to manage and are highly regulated. Burdensome local, state, and federal reports must be filed and regular stockholder meetings must be held.

Continues.

Increased options for growth and fundraising. A corporation has access to numerous investors and can raise substantial capital through the sale of stock.	**Expensive to form and maintain.** The fees for setting up a corporate structure, the costs of stockholders' meetings, and the expense of legal fees and paperwork are some of the costs unique to the corporation.
The corporation is a separate entity. It is responsible and liable for all debts. The shareholders are liable only for the amount they have invested. The corporation has an existence apart from the people who own it.	**Increased tax load.** Income tax is paid on the corporate net income (profit) and on individual salaries and dividends.
Authority can be delegated. The corporation has the ability to draw on the expertise and skills of more than one individual.	

Because of the complexity of this type of business, you may wish to consult a lawyer regarding its formation. Whether you choose to form the corporation on your own or with legal help, you have to consider the following items in order to be knowledgeable and prepared.

WHY INCORPORATE?

Accountants and lawyers encourage you to incorporate. Other than lawyers benefiting from their fees and accountants getting more work to do when you incorporate, there is always a question whether you should incorporate. Weigh the pros (e.g., limiting your liability in case you get sued) and cons (paying more taxes) depending on your situation. Incorporate if it is to your advantage; and incorporate when you wish to.

CERTIFICATE OF INCORPORATION

Preparing a certificate of incorporation is generally the first step to incorporating. Many states use a standard certificate of incorporation form that may be used by small businesses. Copies may be obtained from the state official who grants charters or from larger stationers or office suppliers.

The following information is required:

- **Name of the corporation.** Choose a name that must not be the same as or similar to any other corporation authorized to do business in the state. Your name must not be deceptive so as to mislead the public. To be certain that the name you select is suitable, check the name availability through the designated state official in each state in which you intend to do business before drawing up the certificate of incorporation.
- **Purposes for which the corporation is formed.** Your purposes should be broad enough to allow for expansion and specific enough to give a clear idea of the business you perform. Reference books and certificates of existing corporations are available at your local library and can provide examples of such clauses.
- **Length of time for which the corporation will exist.** The period of time you plan to operate your corporation may vary— terms may cover a fixed number of years or it could be "perpetual."
- **Names and addresses of incorporators.** In some areas, at least one or more of your incorporators is required to be a resident of the state in which your corporation is being organized.
- **Location of the registered office of the corporation in the state of the incorporation.** If you decide to obtain your charter from another state, you are required to have an office there. You may appoint an agent in that state to act for you.
- **Proposed capital structure.** State the maximum amount and type of capital stock your corporation wishes authorization to issue. State the amount of capital required at the time of incorporation.
- **Management.** State the provisions for regulating the internal affairs of the corporation.
- **Director.** Provide the name and address of the person who will serve as your director until the first meeting of the stockholders.

The charter will be issued if and when the designated state official determines that the name is available, that the certificate has been completely and properly executed, and that no violation of state law has occurred.

Suzanne said that in bringing her status of "Approved Independent Contractor" up to date, she learned that some clients require some or all of the following Incorporation and Business documents: Statement of Work (SOW) or description of services provided for the project, stamped copy of Articles or Certificate of Incorporation, Certificate of Insurance that complies with certain limits, copy of Consulting Agreement, Certificate of Good Standing/Certificate of Existence, if applicable (available from the Secretary of State in the state where you are registered to do business), evidence of other client engagements (1099-S, proposals, SOWs, invoices, contracts, etc.), proof that your employees are paid on Form W-2 (if applicable) and that your insurance covers them, copies of all business or professional licenses (if applicable), copy of my invoice form that is normally used to bill for services, and other evidence of ongoing business, such as marketing materials, brochures, publications, white papers, press releases, customer lists, and many more.

KEY POINTS

- Realize the type of consultant you are, what your contract requirements are, and how each dictates how you spend time at your home office, on-site, or in other locations.
- Create a list of your consulting services, including your fees/hour for each service. I suggest that you have a range of fees for each of your services representing low, mid-range, high, and very high (for services that are complex and need high-level expertise).
- Understand each contract you accept. Every contract has different approaches and expense procedures, depending on whether you are dealing with a private or a public organization. A public organization (e.g., federal government) may involve more cumbersome expense procedures and a longer payment cycle.
- Find out when to expect payment of invoices you submit.
- Remember that getting started takes the most upfront effort because you have to take many factors into consideration, including set-up, start-up costs, and monthly expenses.

- Know the different rules that apply to you if you are a sole owner, a partner, or a part of a corporation.
- Find out whether you want to incorporate and decide based on your situation.

Chapter Four
Setting Up Your Home Office

Nothing succeeds like address.
—**Fran Lebowitz, author**

Becoming an independent consultant offers you many benefits in addition to the chance to be your own boss, take charge of your life, and get a handle on your destiny. It also offers you the chance to work from home, free from office politics, dress codes, and workplace noise and interruptions. You will love the idea of working at home. You will save time commuting and enjoy having a dedicated office loaded with equipment to run your business.

GETTING SET UP

Working from home is becoming more and more popular. Independent consultants are more in demand as hiring trends change. Yet, you face preparation and planning in getting set up. Part of being your own boss is searching for financing, purchasing necessary equipment, furniture, and supplies, and maintaining your inventory or your skills. Whatever it takes, this is your opportunity to move in a different career direction. There are pros and cons for any type of endeavor you choose, but as long as you prepare and plan well, you will minimize the inevitable bumps along the way. Starting your consulting business is just like starting any other business in that you have to iron out some of the wrinkles as you move on. In time, you will be able to look back fondly at this golden chance to start a new career.

TIME, LOCATION, AND LEVEL OF EFFORT

Depending on the type of consulting work you perform and the unique needs of your clients, you may be able to work from your home office much of the time. If you are a management consultant or are hired to fill a need within a company, these roles involve interacting with others on a frequent basis, and you may find that your workplace is principally "on-site."

Some consultants are paid to create products. In these cases the end product is clearly defined, and little time is required on-site other than for progress reporting or delivering interim products. The consultant is left alone to perform the tasks.

Other consultants provide a physical service for clients in remote locations (such as logistics support services overseas). These consultants might prepare the plan at their home office and then deploy to the geographical region. When the contract period or work is complete, they return home awaiting the next contract assignment. This type of consultant can spend extended periods of time away from home; often, months.

> Frank, who lives in California, spends about 16 days working on the East Coast. He returns home twice monthly to visit family and handle personal and professional business. In my case, I have been fortunate to get projects that let me work from home 95 percent of the time. The remaining five percent I spend attending kick-off meetings, overseeing a pilot test of a training program, meeting with clients to make changes on training programs I designed and developed, or presenting the final training materials for production and delivery to training participants.

It is important to remember that as a consultant, your time is directly related to how much you can earn. Yet you need to perform the kind of administrative functions that are generally performed by non-officers in established companies, such as accounts payable and receivable, information technology, legal, and contracting.

You are your own business as a consultant. Time spent doing personal or other business-related work, is time *not* being spent supporting the client directly. Hence, those tasks must be assigned to the lowest level of staff capable of performing them so you can do the tasks that only you are capable of doing. In addition, until you have clients lined up at your door, you need to develop new business, whether with your current client or others. This may require proposal writing, networking, face-to-face marketing, and endurance. It requires exceptional time management and organizational skills.

Know what the cost of your time is in light of what you need to do to sustain your business. Realize the type of consultant you are, what your contract requirements are, and how all these factors dictate how you will spend time at your home office, on-site, or in other locations.

SPACE

The total amount of space you are going to need to set up a functioning home office depends on the kind of consulting business you plan to engage in and whether you anticipate having clients visit your office. For most consultants, an extra bedroom or a den that can be converted into an office is ideal. In considering the space you need, think about all your furniture, equipment, and supplies. Make sure the room you are going to use is for your business only and nothing else. When I set up my home office, I selected a room to use solely for my business. I had it renovated to make sure that it would have all the conveniences of an office, with built-in bookshelves for books and materials, a comfortable chair and a desk that is also a worktable, and other furniture to hold other equipment, such as printer, copier, and fax machine. I added shelves in a former walk-in closet for office supplies and bookshelves for my resource books and materials. Because my office is self-contained, I do not have to wander to other rooms to find supplies or equipment I'd need. When I need privacy, I can just close my door.

Some key points to consider in using a space in your house for your office:

- Ensure that your space is one that lets you focus on your work. It should be situated in a convenient location. If you have a family, avoid having your home office located in the middle of your family's traffic pattern, where daily activities such as children getting ready to go to school or a spouse rushing off to work, occur.

- Easy access that won't disturb your household. It helps to have a separate entrance other than your front door if possible, especially if you expect clients to visit you in your home office or frequent delivery of goods.
- Make sure your space is livable. If you are going to spend a lot of time in your home office, make it comfortable and inviting. Have adequate heat and plenty of cool air whenever you need it. Have blinds or drapes that can control the amount of outside light entering your office. Select décor that is both easy on the eyes and practical.
- Have good lighting, whether natural or artificial, with both overhead lights and desk lamps. In my own home office, which has two big windows and enough lighting coming in from the outside, I have only a desk lamp and recessed lights located close to the bookshelves. This allows me to easily find books and other materials I need at night.
- Make sure your office is well ventilated. This is especially necessary if you have computers, printers, copiers, and other office equipment that generates heat, dust, and ozone.
- Have plenty of grounded electric receptacles for your equipment, phone, lamps, radio, and anything else you need. You do not want to see wires running across your room; that could be a fire hazard as well as an eyesore. You may want to invest in additional electrical outlets.
- Consider having a home security system installed, especially if you have a lot of equipment. The system can be tied to an alarm or monitoring service. You might consider buying a small fireproof safe to store your disks, tapes, or other media.

FURNITURE AND FIXTURES

Your office might contain more than a desk and a chair. You might want to fully equip your office with furniture and the latest technology depending on the type of consulting you do. You don't have to buy everything new. Look for used furniture or rent furniture if you don't have ready cash to spend. You can also surf web sites like eBay for used computers and software at affordable prices.

Some practical furniture you might want to consider:

- **A chair.** Get an ergonomically correct chair since you will probably spend a lot of time at your computer. You know how important it is to sit in a healthful working position. In the past, I didn't think that the height of my chair was important for working at my computer. I realized the problem only when I developed tendinitis in my wrists.
- **A desk.** Think about what you are going to put on your desk. Computer, printer, phone, calculator, file boxes, and calendars. You need ample space to accommodate everything plus allow you sufficient working space for writing or reading or laying out materials for review. If you have enough office space, set up extra work surfaces or buy a large desk that can serve multiple purposes.
- **Worktables.** A couple of these are useful so you don't cramp your desk with everything. These will also help you organize. Worktables do not have to be fancy. You can even get simple tables with folding legs, so you can fold and stash them in a corner or a closet.
- **File cabinets.** If you deal with a large volume of paperwork as part of your consulting practice, you need filing space. An organized filing system is critical to your efficiency, so think carefully about how you will set up your filing and record-keeping systems before you plunge into consulting. My filing cabinet, for example, is located close to my desk, and its folders are alphabetically arranged by subject for easy reference. For record-keeping, I suggest you get a three-ring binder with a set of dividers that you can label with the key elements of your start-up activities. These could include networking/contacts, consulting ideas, marketing techniques, expenses, financing, business plans, insurance, taxes, and retirement plans. Record-keeping is an integral part of setting up your office.
- **Bookshelves.** These are useful for a variety of purposes, such as to store business-oriented computer software, books, magazines,

a laptop computer, display of completed products or projects, and more.

- **Storage space.** Set aside a cabinet, drawers, or closet shelves to hold your office supplies, like computer paper (which is cheaper to buy 10 reams at a time), pens, pencils, paper clips, stapler with matching staples, envelopes, and so on. The advantage of having separate storage for supplies is that it simplifies seeing which supplies need replenishment.

EQUIPMENT AND SUPPLIES

Other than furniture, you need certain pieces of equipment and supplies to run your consulting practice. You can start with basic equipment and add on as your business grows or as your needs change.

- **Telephone.** Add a landline ("wired line") separate from the home phone. Or you can add multiple lines and a speakerphone. If you need a phone away from home, get a cell phone or a wireless unit. Don't forget to have an answering machine or a service so your clients can leave messages when you're not available. The advantage of having this extra phone line is that you do not have to keep switching between phone and fax. A landline business phone helps you to keep your business in the office where it belongs and not in your pocket (cell phone) 24/7. Also, you get the highest-quality voice transmission; dropped calls can never be an issue with a landline. The cost of a landline used exclusively for business is 100 percent deductible. Extra features you'll need include: voice mail, call waiting, and caller ID. Most companies include these as part of their monthly bundled service package, although you may have to pay a little extra for voice mail (usually around $2 to $5 monthly). If you add an extra line for your fax machine or modem, you may be able to get a multi-line discount.
- **Computer.** Get the best you can afford and make sure it comes with the kinds of software you need for your line of work. If you work primarily at home, get a standard desktop computer. If you travel a lot, get a laptop computer. Check computer stores for exactly what you will need, depending on the services you provide.

- **Fax/scanner/printer/copier (all-in-one) machine.** Consider a multipurpose machine that can also fax, scan, print, and copy. You can find these all-in-one machines in many chain stores such as Office Depot, Office Max, Staples, Best Buy, Sam's Club, Costco, Walmart, and some others.
- **Internet access.** If you're new to the Internet, sign up with an established online service, such as America OnLine (AOL), Cox Communications, Comcast or an online service specific only to your area. You get unlimited access to the Internet and the World Wide Web for very reasonable monthly flat rates, which let you also send and receive as much email as you like. If you are a senior citizen, ask about their senior rates. Also consider asking your cable provider for bundled service, where you can purchase service for telephone and Internet for a reasonable rate.

Depending on the volume of work that you do, it may be advisable to subscribe to an online Digital Subscriber Line, commonly known as DSL. DSL is a fast, efficient method of sending data through existing telephone lines rather than via modem-to-modem communications. Quick advantages for you are that: your computer is always on; you do not have to dial up; you don't tie up your phone line; and, networking hardware lets you share the service. What you get are high-speed Internet access and value-added services. Monthly service is reasonable and could cost you as little as $29.95, with no setup or equipment fees. The top ten DSL providers for both residential and business use are Verizon, AT&T, SBC Southwestern Bell, Sprint, SBC Pacific Bell, Bell South, SBC Prodigy, Covad, QWest, and XO. Each of these providers covers different regions. For instance, SBC Pacific Bell only covers California. In a November 7, 2012 press release posted on technobuffalo.com, AT&T currently has global Internet-Protocol based network capabilities, and they will invest $14 billion to significantly expand and enhance its wireless and broadband networks to support growing customer demand. That is why you have to do some research for coverage and cost before you make a decision in subscribing to a particular DSL. For more information on rates, fees, contract length, and current coverage from these top ten DSLs, go to www.billsaver.com. If you live in an area that only allows you a Dial-Up Service, cost is one-half the price of a DSL.

- **Office Supplies.** You need essentials such as pens and pencils (to include colored markers and yellow highlighters), paper (letter- or legal-sized paper, ruled pads, 24-pound paper for use to send to clients, plain-paper or laser printer paper), fastening devices (staples, paper clips), mailing envelopes (#10 envelopes, 9-x-12 inch or 10-x-13 inch) and folders (different sizes, colors, and types), sticky notes, and a good supply of your business cards.

  Keep track of computer equipment, software, furniture, and other fixed assets in a separate expense category. When it comes to work on depreciation expenses, you'll need to know when a particular piece of equipment was purchased as well as its cost and the type of equipment that was purchased.

INSURANCE

Wearing your entrepreneurial hat, you are responsible for getting the insurance coverage you need. Be careful that you are neither under-insured nor over-insured. If you run across insurance agents who are articulate and have sales savvy, they might convince you to buy insurance you don't need. Play it safe. Check all possibilities. Ask questions but don't let an insurance agent make the decisions for you. If an agent cannot answer all the questions you need answered, it is time to look elsewhere.

Commit yourself to getting the insurance you need when you feel comfortable making your decision. The types of insurance you might need will vary according to your consulting needs and your situation. For information on getting insurance rates online, refer to Chapter 9.

Here are some of the most important types of insurance to get:

- **Overhead expense insurance**
  If your business income were to stop if illness or an accident temporarily disabled you, you need to buy overhead expense insurance. This covers the costs of fixed business expenses that must be met even when you are unable to generate income.

- **Personal disability insurance**
  You need to consider the effect of becoming disabled for a short or long period of time. Personal disability insurance pays you a certain monthly amount if you are permanently disabled, or a portion of that amount if you are partially disabled but capable of generating some income. (Sometimes this is not available to sole proprietors who work at home.)
- **Health (medical) insurance**
  It is important to take out sufficient medical coverage for your needs. If you are working solo and accept consulting assignments outside the country, you should get extended insurance. Getting health insurance is a major concern and problem for many self-employed people, especially those who work alone.

  Individual rates are priced higher than group rates. If you are married and your spouse has health insurance, you can have him or her include you as a dependent. This way the insurance premium will be affordable. (Perhaps consider liability insurance if clients come to your home.) This turned out to be in my favor since my spouse includes me as a dependent so I don't have an added expense or medical insurance.

  If you are aged fifty or above, join the American Association of Retired Persons (AARP) or any of many professional organizations in your field that offer insurance plans to senior citizens. If you have a few employees, your best option is to get group insurance through some association. Check the more appropriate carriers in the yellow pages of your telephone directory, or ask friends if they can refer you to reputable companies.

  If you are self-employed and pay for your own health insurance, then you can deduct the full cost of your health insurance premiums on your Form 1040 as a personal deduction. In order to deduct your health insurance expenses, you must have a net profit from your business. If you have zero profit or a net loss, you can still deduct the health insurance premiums. Also, you cannot deduct if your spouse is covered by an employer-provided plan. My spouse is covered by an employer-provided plan so I cannot deduct my health insurance premiums.

As a self-employed consultant, health insurance is Suzanne's greatest business expense. Obviously, the selection of a particular type of coverage and policy will vary greatly, but even the lower-cost options can take a giant bite out of earnings. Her personal experience for the past several years is that health insurance premiums cost roughly one-fifth of her consulting gross income. Of course, this is accommodated as a business expense in her federal income taxes, 1040 Schedule C, which is then computed into the calculation of her Self-Employment tax.

If you were laid off, an option is to get a COBRA (Consolidated Omnibus Budget Reconciliation Act). COBRA requires companies with twenty or more employees to allow you to stay on your health plan for an additional eighteen months after you leave your job. Of course, the downside is that you are responsible for your premiums; COBRA is a good option for you while you are not yet earning or just starting your consulting career. You may shop for temporary insurance coverage, which may be less expensive than a COBRA; check with an insurance carrier for the best option for a less expensive or more affordable monthly premium.

- **Term life insurance**
  Term life insurance is the most basic life insurance that provides financial protection for a specified time, such as ten or fifteen years. It is simple (if the insured dies, the policyholder pays out the stated death benefit to the beneficiaries; this is relatively inexpensive) and you can carry it for the time in your life when you need it most, such as while you have children living at home and while you have a mortgage on your home; it is readily available and straightforward. I decided to get term life insurance coverage five years ago for a term of ten years. I checked the website for possible insurance agencies and decided on Prudential Insurance and contacted an agent in my area. It was a quick process. After the agent arranged for a medical check-up, which was done by sending someone to my house, the process continued with forms signed, beneficiaries assigned, and coverage started. With this coverage, if I die within ten years of buying the policy, my insurance company pays the full-face amount to my beneficiaries. The

downside is that when the term life insurance expires (in my case, only five years remain), there is no cash or savings value built up in the account. If your financial resources are limited currently, you should purchase term life insurance to protect your family and be able to assign your beneficiaries. Some insurance providers often allow you to convert your term life to whole life insurance although your premium will be much higher.

- **Whole life insurance or permanent life insurance**
  Whole life insurance provides long-term financial protection in two ways: It provides a lifetime coverage at a premium that *never* changes, and it can grow a cash value that can be borrowed against or cashed in. Purchase the whole life insurance if you can afford it because the coverage is for your entire life with fixed premiums. Depending on your plan, you can withdraw some or all of the value you have built in the policy or use the dividends to pay part of your premiums. The whole life insurance can be "forced savings" protecting your family's future and your benefit can be taken as monthly payments instead of a lump sum payment.

- **Professional liability insurance (or errors and omissions insurance)**
  Professional liability insurance protects you from financial losses if a client sues you for alleged negligence in rendering professional service or providing advice. This is one of the most common types of specialized liability insurance that is always sold separately as a specialized insurance specific to the nature of the profession. In some states, this type of insurance is mandatory. It used to be that only practicing professionals like lawyers, doctors, accountants, and engineers carry professional liability insurance. Now, it is common for almost every type of business professional and consultant, such as advertising and marketing consultants, software developers, webmasters—just to name a few.

  Obtaining professional liability insurance is a relatively straightforward process (just like term life insurance). Begin by checking your specific professional organizations or associations because many offer insurance programs for their members. You can also ask your current insurance agent to recommend an agent who specializes in liability insurance coverage. American professional agency provides free professional liability quotes on its website. Go to www.americanprofessional.com and check out the site. It is indexed by type of profession and then indexed geographically by state.

Suzanne was required to obtain business and professional insurances and provide evidence to include the following items (Note: Dollar amounts are what were required from her current client; other clients may require different levels of insurance liability): workers' compensation insurance (if required by law) with statutory limits and employers' liability insurance with a limit of not less than $1,000,000; consultant agrees to waive all rights of subrogation against client; comprehensive general liability insurance, including contractual coverage, product, and completed operations coverage, and broad form vendors coverage with a combined single limit of not less than $5,000,000, alone or in combination with Excess Umbrella Liability coverage; if use of a vehicle is a required part of the services provided, Automotive Liability Insurance with a combined single limit of $5,000,000, alone or in combination with Excess Umbrella Liability coverage; Errors and Omissions coverage with minimum limits of $1,000,000. In Suzanne's case, the client required that the insurance policies list them as an additional insured on all liability policies.

RETIREMENT PLANS

It is important to put away money for your later years when you cannot or don't want to work quite so hard. Like other goals you may have, retirement planning begins with a vision of the future that gets translated into weekly, monthly, or annual goals.

You will find it easy to ignore retirement planning as you move through the first years of consulting. You always put it off for another day—until you realize it may be too late to start. If you start late, your retirement money may not be enough to cover your daily expenses.

Financial specialists tell you that when you retire, you need 60 to 80 percent of your final annual income every year. Postponing retirement planning only robs you of the time to compound your savings.

You can set up your retirement plan with a financial institution of your choice or work with a qualified retirement specialist. If you already have either of these, they can give you the yearly contribution limits. The IRS Publication 590 (individual retirement arrangements) is updated on an annual basis so you can also check the information against this government resource, or go to www.irs.gov/pub/irs-pdf/p590.pdf.

- **Simplified Employee Plan - Individual Retirement Account (SEP-IRA)**
  SEPs are pretty much like IRAs. The difference is the amount of money you are permitted to contribute. SEP-IRA is the best choice if you are working by yourself or just starting out, because it is easy to set up and maintain. You can contribute flexible amounts each year, up to $50,000 in 2012 (or 25 percent of your net earnings from self-employment), whichever is less.
- **Keogh Plan**
  Another option is a Keogh plan, sometimes called the qualified plan or HR10 plan. Keogh plans allow self-employed individuals the opportunity for retirement savings benefits and their rules are quite different from the IRA's. It allows you to put money aside each year to use in retirement. In 2012, the contribution limit increased to $50,000 (or 25 percent of your eligible compensation). A Keogh requires much more paperwork, but it also has advantages. Keogh is more complicated and is designed for those with higher, more stable incomes.
- **Other sources of retirement plans**
  These plans require you to have, before you go into consulting, a retirement savings plan from your previous employer, such as tax-favored plan like a 401(k).

401(k) plans are retirement accounts. You set aside a percentage of your compensation on a before-tax basis through regular payroll deductions. Employers normally provide discretionary matching contributions to help increase your participation in the plan. Salary deferrals are $17,000 in 2012 plus an additional $5,500 if you're fifty or older. To benefit you the most, tailor your plan to allow you access to the money in the plan through loans and hardship distributions. The one major restriction is that you must leave the accumulated money in the account until you are fifty-nine and a half years of age or face a penalty upon early withdrawal, although you can draw the money for hardship reasons without penalty. However, before you quit your job to become an independent consultant, you must tell your employer that you want a direct rollover into an IRA.

IRAs are Individual Retirement Accounts. These are available to all working Americans and are especially attractive to those who work for companies that do not offer retirement savings plans. Self-employed consultants can defer paying taxes on the income used to acquire an IRA until the retirement years put you in a lower tax bracket.

Ultimately, just like planning for anything, you need to really research these retirement plans. Work with a financial planner to find out the best plan for you.

KEY ISSUES THAT MIGHT ENDANGER TAKING A HOME OFFICE DEDUCTION

One question new consultants ask is how to receive a home office tax deduction. Tax cuts for a home-based office can be a benefit but they are also one of the most misunderstood aspects of tax obligations and deductions. Deductions should only be made for business expenses. The government is very particular about exactly who is eligible to take the home-office deduction and under what circumstances. Writing off a part of your home as a business raises a red flag for the IRS. It is wise to consult with the IRS or a tax advisor so you are sure you know what you are doing.

For instance, as an independent consultant, I do not include my home office space as a deduction because of the strict IRS guidelines. I only deduct expenses like office equipment and supplies, business lunches, and gas expenses for meeting potential and existing clients.

Consider these points from the National Federation of Independent Business (NFIB):

1. First, measure your "home office percentage." This is the percentage of most household expenses, including utilities and housekeeping, which you can deduct. The ratio is: your home office's square footage divided by the total square footage of your home, measured internal wall-to-wall.

2. Measure your home office space accurately. During a popular small business webinar on 2012 tax planning sponsored by NFIB, presenter Cliff Enrico suggested paying for a contractor to make this measurement. Why? You want this calculation to be as accurate as possible. By hiring a professional, you'll receive a precise number and written documentation. Many do-it-yourselfers underestimate the percentage, which leads to underestimating the deductions they are entitled to.

3. Keep personal effects out of your office so you don't lose the deduction. Remember, your home office is dedicated business space, so don't use it for non-business purposes. Pictures of family—that's acceptable. A small boom box to listen to music or news—that's reasonable. A crib? A doggie bed? These are definite no-nos as they are items you wouldn't have in a regular office. Such personal effects will stick out during an audit (if you happen to get audited), making it appear that the space in question is not used exclusively and regularly for business purposes.

4. Don't deduct home office expenses for things that take place outside of the home. The costs for services such as landscaping, lawn care, and tree care are not deductible.

5. Include storage and warehouse spacing in your calculation—but only the amount you are using for business. If you use part of your basement for storing inventory or office supplies, you can't count the entire basement as part of your home office deduction. Cliff Enrico suggests one option to delineate the storage area in a basement: duct tape. Mark off the section of the floor that is used exclusively for business storage. If a tax agent ever comes to your home to investigate, it will be immediately obvious which section of your basement you have dedicated for business.

6. Don't deduct someone else's office space, even if you store inventory or office supplies there. Deduction only applies to your own home. If you have a neighbor or friend who lets you use their

space, you can explore an alternative approach. Have a lawyer draw up a formal lease spelling out the agreement and then pay rent on a per square foot basis. You can then deduct the rent payment as an ordinary and necessary business expense.

TIPS AND STRATEGIES FOR TAXES

There are special circumstances that apply to an independent or self-employed consultant. As self-employed, you are in full control of your financial and tax situation, and you face higher taxes and more record-keeping duties than if you were an employee.

The IRS routinely audits independent consultants, often looking for unreported income or overstated deductions—know exactly what can and can't be deducted. Understand basic tax planning for independent consultants, which is substantially different from taxes for full-time employees.

As an independent consultant, you are taxed on your net self-employment income (net after various business expenses have been deducted from your gross income). Also, you generally do not have taxes deducted from your pay (unlike employees), so you need to remit tax payments periodically throughout the year using Form 1040-ES for estimated taxes. A typical tax planning strategy begins by keeping track of income and expenses, calculating estimated taxes, and then making financial decisions that might reduce taxes to a desired level. Estimated tax payments to federal and state governments might not show up clearly if you run an expense report just for the calendar year, as the final estimated payment is due in January.

As self-employed, you are required to file an annual return and pay estimated tax quarterly. You must pay a self-employment (SE) tax as well as an income tax. SE tax is a Social Security and Medicare tax primarily for individuals who work for themselves. Before you can determine if you are subject to self-employment tax and income tax, you must figure your net profit or net loss from your business. You can do this by subtracting your business expenses from your business income. If your expenses are less than your income, the difference is net profit and becomes part of your income on page 1 of Form 1040. If your expenses are more than your income, the difference is a net loss. You usually do not deduct your loss from gross income but in some situations your loss is limited.

The SE tax is 15.3 percent of your net profit and represents the Social Security and Medicare taxes owed on your business profit. As an employee (on a W-2 form), you only pay half of the Social Security and Medicare taxes (7.65 percent), and your employer pays the other half. As a freelancer or an independent consultant, you are your own employer, so you pay both halves. For your convenience, you can enroll in EFTPS (Electronic Federal Tax Payment System). It takes some time to get set up with the EFTPS, but once you're fully registered with the website, you can make estimated tax payments by phone or by web, with the payment debited directly from your checking account.

Making Quarterly Payments. Estimated tax is the method used to pay Social Security and Medicare taxes and income tax, because you do not have an employer withholding these taxes for you. Use Form 1040-ES Estimated Tax for Individuals. You will need your prior year's annual tax return in order to fill out Form 1040-ES.

Filing an Annual Return. To file your annual tax return, you will need to use Schedule C-EZ to report your income or loss from a business you operated or a profession you practiced as sole proprietor or independent consultant.

For more information on tax estimates and payments go to www.irs.gov/businesses.

KEY POINTS

- Know the cost of your time in light of what you need to do to set up your home office.
- Understand the specifics on how to get yourself set up: the time, location, and level of your overall effort; amount of space you need to be able to work comfortably in your own home office; the kind of furniture and fixtures, equipment and supplies to acquire; kinds of insurance you need or your client requires as a condition of approving your contract; a good retirement plan to prepare you for the future, and so on.
- Know how to build your business—not just for today but also for the future.
- Plan your resources well. It takes time once you've begun work as a consultant to get paid, so having a minimum of six months of

your equivalent salary in the bank will help you feel less pressure to accept the first consulting job that comes your way.

- Keep in mind that taking the step to becoming an independent consultant isn't easy; it takes a lot of hard work, patience, and endurance.
- Remember that continuously updating your skills, especially in technology, helps to keep you marketable.
- Be aware of issues that might hinder taking a home office deduction.
- Make sure you follow the tips and strategies for estimating, calculating, and keeping track of your taxes and tax payments.
- Know the laws concerning payments to be made as an independent consultant or a sole proprietor, and make sure to check the IRS website for exact information and forms you will need.
- Check out retirement plans that will fit your financial situation.

Chapter Five
Using Social Media to Market Services

Social marketing eliminates the middlemen, providing brands the unique opportunity to have a direct relationship with their customers.
—**Bryan Weiner, CEO of Digital Agency 360i**

Social media has become a popular means of communication (for personal or business use). Social media platforms are now very often used to market products and services, but to get wider exposure to potential clients, it is wise for consultants to use a combination of social media and traditional marketing approaches. See Chapter 8 for information on traditional marketing approaches.

Social media: A group of new kinds of online media, which share most or all of the following characteristics: participation, openness, conversation, community, and connectedness.

Purpose: Users can easily participate in, share, and create content, including blogs, social networks, wikis, forums, and virtual worlds.

GUIDE TO GET STARTED
Social media should be part of your marketing strategy. These steps will help you get started:

Step 1: Choose the platforms. Which ones should you use? This partly depends on the demographic of your target audience. Start by writing a blog (using a platform like WordPress or Blogger) and create your profile on LinkedIn, Facebook, and Twitter. You do not have to manage all of these, as cross-platform integration will help.

Step 2: Connect. Start by connecting with your friends and colleagues on LinkedIn, Facebook, and Twitter. Your selected network will hopefully share your content with their networks. Then search and connect/follow anyone that falls into your target audience. Use the search functionality on these sites to find people that are commenting on the consulting services you are offering.

Step 3: Create content. Make sure that your content is not boring or stale. Write blog posts on niche, yet interesting topics, crammed with keywords that people are likely to search. Try searching "top marketing trends 2012" for example.

Step 4: Share. Now that you have your content, it's time to share it. You may only have a few LinkedIn connections, but that doesn't matter; you can search out your target audience and share your content with new contacts.

Step 5: Become an authority. Social authority is developed when you establish yourself as an "expert" in your given field, thereby becoming an influence in that field.

Step 6: Be Patient. Don't expect immediate results —persevere.

Step 7: Engage. If someone has taken the time to reply to your message or posted a comment relating to your social media activity, then reply back. Reply with links to other posts of yours or invite them to follow or connect with you in other social media networks. Social media is as much about engagement as it is about anything else —it shouldn't be underestimated.

SOCIAL MEDIA PLATFORMS

You shouldn't use just one single platform to support your marketing efforts, and it is unlikely that your potential clients will only use one platform either. Your clients may use two or more platforms to post their profiles since it is not that much more expensive to market on one than to market on several.

Where do you market? Since it takes time and effort to put your marketing efforts together, select just one that best meet your needs or a few social media platforms where your potential clients participate the most. To pick the right platforms, look at audiences with which you interact, particularly clients and industry.

Clients should be your main targets. You want to connect, interact, and prompt them to use your services so you should research which platforms your clients will most likely be using. Use tools like Quantcast (www.quantcast.com) to help you understand how each social media site works and how to optimize traffic on your page, although you may have to research each social platform's site to understand the details of engaging with your target audience on it.

LinkedIn, Facebook, Twitter, and blogs are industry-specific and well known, and are the most commonly used for marketing.

LinkedIn may still be the best place to do your marketing because clients most commonly use LinkedIn to ask each other for advice related to business and business decisions.

You shouldn't rule out other outlets though. Facebook offers the option of creating a fan page for a company or product and is a good way to engage clients in discussions.

Twitter is a microblogging service that lets you tweet 140-character messages, and only people who follow you see your tweets in their stream. When you market on Twitter, focus more on building relationships that will potentially lead to creating business relationships.

Blogs are online journals written by users and are helpful in spreading news and information. YouTube is a repository for podcasts and video clips, with a viewership of millions around the globe. You can make a video showcasing your skills or thoughts, and spread your name. Each of these platforms allows you to post links of your other platforms and sites and create a web centered around your consulting business.

Meryl has experience with some of these platforms and explains:

> I use Facebook mostly for personal contacts, but I have some business contacts there as well. LinkedIn is a tool I'm not using as effectively as I would like, but I know of others

who like LinkedIn as they can get business connections through previous employers and colleagues. Marketing is hard work. Sometimes it takes years of keeping in touch to generate business.

Consulting service is not cut and dried. In addition to using social media platforms to keep up with your existing and potential clients, you will need traditional marketing approaches, like networking. People need to get to know you and trust you to do a good job. Social media is great for keeping in touch but establishing relationships using networking, for instance, is a key to success.

A friend of mine blogs for the *Huffington Post Weekly*, and she is very honored to be able to do this, a testament of the willpower of a consultant to think outside the box (and ask for work) to get work. Blogging is an unpaid task, but the advantage is that you get your name and services out there and get noticed. You can also use your business as your tagline and include a link to make it easy for readers to find out about your services.

In contrast to Meryl, independent-consultant Laurence does not use social media to market his services. He said that he is "old school" and prefers to continue using traditional marketing approaches (like networking and word-of-mouth referrals) and, so far, these have been sufficient for him.

ADVANTAGES OF USING SOCIAL MEDIA

Social media has become indispensable as a marketing strategy tool for consultants, because it is the best way to reach clients. Advantages include:

1. Low cost: Most social media platforms are free to access and allow you to create profile and post information. You can reach your target audience for little or no cash investment. Pay-per-click advertisements on sites such as Facebook are "geo-targeted" according to specific criteria, and help you reach a niche audience. The viral nature of social media means that each person who reads your posts has the capability to spread the news farther within his own network, so information can reach a large number of people in a short time.

2. Unlimited access: Most social media networks are accessible to anyone and everyone.

3. Simplicity: Social media channels are extremely simple to use, even for people with basic information technology (IT) experience; all that is required is a computer and an Internet connection.

4. Global reach: You can communicate information in a flash, regardless of geographical location. Social media platforms also allow you to tailor your content to your targeted market and give you the opportunity to get your message across more quickly and widely than using traditional media. For example, if one piece of content goes viral, there is no limit to the amount of people it could potentially reach, all at no extra cost to you.

5. Contact building: Social media channels offer unparalleled opportunities for you to interact and build relationships with your clients because they are real-time and interactive. For example, Facebook gives you the chance to select the type and frequency of messages to receive and send out.

> Meryl uses *Constant Contact*, which is a nice tool for keeping in touch with clients. She can provide clients with great little tidbits or articles about what she is planning, projects she is working on or planning to work on, and even sends them personal information—a great marketing tool. She uses *Webstart Communications* for her own personal website. *Webstart Communications* focuses on web content and advertising.

6. Flexibility: Information can be updated, altered, supplemented, and discussed in a way that is not possible in a printed advertisement, a newspaper article, or magazine feature.

7. Measurability: You can test the most effective marketing messages and approaches, gauge user responses, and tweak your messages accordingly. This is done through the ever-growing number of free, easy-to-use social media measurement tools, such as Google Analytics and Delicious.

DISADVANTAGES OF USING SOCIAL MEDIA

1. Time and effort: Updating your social media accounts takes some time, especially if you really want it to work. It takes effort to find new angles for promoting your consulting services continually and to post and re-post information.

2. Short time visibility: Your information is only visible for a short time before newer posts replace it. In addition, publishing obvious advertising copy is looked down upon in the social media world, therefore, you must present the information in the form of conversation or you will lose followers.

SOCIAL MEDIA MARKETING RISKS

Social media marketing carries several risks. Unless you have someone check your social media accounts several times a day, disgruntled clients or employees can publish negative comments that are not always removable. For example, every post on Twitter is public and you have no control over what people say. Bad news can go viral just as easily as good news and can irreparably harm your business. The IT Governance group (the Information Systems Audit and Control Association) released a report in June 2010 ranking viruses and malware, brand hijacking, lack of control over corporate content, unrealistic customer expectations, and non-compliance with record management regulations as the top five risks of social media.

BUILDING YOUR SOCIAL MEDIA PROFILE

A profile is a collection of facts about you. Creating a profile is easy and the information you provide depends on what you want your network members to know about you and your services, if you decide to place an ad to market your service using any of these platforms.

A few social media platforms are available for free or at a low cost. Three of the most popular based on their size and growth rate are: LinkedIn, Facebook, and Twitter.

- **LinkedIn**
  The LinkedIn profile enables people to connect and reconnect with you, presents your career accomplishments, opens a door to new opportunities, and helps you control your professional identity online. LinkedIn is different from other major social media platforms in that it is focused exclusively on work and business-related issues. It provides a way for like-minded business people to find each other, share information, and give advice.

- **Facebook**
  All your Facebook friends and fellow network members can see your profile details (except for those you explicitly exclude). Facebook automatically creates a bare-bones profile for you based on the information you enter when you register. Whether or not you add additional details is up to you. When you refine your Facebook profile, ask yourself three questions: What do I want to get out of Facebook? How security-conscious am I? How much time do I want to spend on this?

  In the May 14, 2012 issue of *USA Today*, Facebook announced an update to its data-use policy in an attempt to give people more clarity on how the company uses information that users share. According to the article, "The policy changes are in response to an audit by Irish data-protection authorities [in 2011]. The commission had asked Facebook to be more transparent about how it collects people's data and uses it for advertising, as well as how long it keeps such information." Facebook's chief privacy officer, Erin Egan, said that "the company wasn't substantially changing its business practices, but wants to err on the side of providing too much information." The site has a section explaining exactly how it uses technologies to make the site secure, deliver ads, and provide other features and will keep information "as long as it is necessary to provide services" as opposed to the 180-day standard before. Early in 2012, many news outlets published the results of a poll done by the Associated Press and CNBC showing that half of Americans think Facebook is a passing fad, while, 57 percent of users say that they never click on the site's ads, and 25 percent say they never do. Many people distrust the security of the ads regardless of the popularity of the site.

- **Twitter**
  The "bio" box allows for 140 characters to tell your life story. You can do it in a series of words or phrases, like John Smith: "Independent Computer Consultant, Certified and Licensed in state-of-the-art hardware and software packages, twenty years of computer industry experience."

SOCIAL MEDIA MARKETING DEFINED

Social media marketing is a process that uses *social media* (content created by everyday people using highly accessible and scalable technologies, such as blogs, message boards, bookmarks, social networks, communities, wikis, and vlogs) to attract attention and traffic for a business.

ROLE OF MARKETER

When marketing your consulting business, you need to:

1. Persuade—Persuasion is your most important tool. You persuade your potential client to use your services.
2. Utilize distribution channels—Social media platforms only do half the work to get people's attention. To get additional opportunities, you need to link to other distribution channels (blogs, websites, newsletters), and use these for your marketing campaign.
3. Create content—You need an editorial calendar, which shows your services, for instance. Having your information on the web is key to getting your existing and potential clients to visit often.
4. Be prepared to experiment and change direction—You can change direction of your marketing campaign based on feedback you get from clients. Start small before expanding to a full-blown campaign.

To market your services, you can use Facebook for professional networking and for tapping into your friends' expertise and contacts.

There is no set cost for an ad on Facebook. Instead, you specify a maximum amount you are willing to spend on an ad either on a "per click" or "per thousand impressions" basis. Facebook shows your ad in places where it is contextually relevant to the theme of your ad. The current minimum for "per click" is $0.01; minimum for "per thousand impressions" is $0.02.

To advertise on Facebook: Click on the "advertising" link in the footer of the Facebook home page.

1. From this page, click the green "create an ad" button.
2. On the next screen, you'll be able to design your ad. A Facebook ad contains three main elements: the destination URL, the link, and the body of the ad. Your Facebook ad will be seen by people who will most likely be interested in your consulting services. However, one disadvantage of advertising on Facebook is the fact that a big portion of their users are high school students, college students, and college-educated people. You certainly can't only use Facebook if you need to reach everyone around retirement age, for instance.

To advertise on LinkedIn (steps to install widget):

1. On your home page, click the "developers" link in the Tools Menu in the Navigation Footer; then click the "get started" link under the LinkedIn widgets section. Click the "get the code" link under the "share on LinkedIn" section of the page.
2. The widget produces a URL encoded with parameters including URL, Title, Summary, and Source, which are populated when a user shares that piece of content.
3. Paste the URL into the source code of each page, where you want your widget to appear.

If you want to venture into *video marketing*, make sure you understand scripting models, sample concepts, video development, and production. If you want to enhance your marketing strategies, video marketing is an option but it is not an easy or fast process as writing an ad and posting it. It requires an effective video marketing strategy, thorough planning, and serious thought on what you want to convey. To promote your services using video marketing, you have to resort to using blogging, email lists, pay-per-view (through TV, which could be costly), and social media sites. This approach may not be ideal for new consultants as it can turn into an expensive and time-consuming feat.

COMPARING SOCIAL MEDIA MARKETING VERSUS TRADITIONAL MARKETING

Social media and traditional marketing approaches are different yet similar in a lot of ways. The philosophies and ideas behind marketing is primarily the same but different in the way results are achieved.

- You have to target the right audience. The "one size fits all" approach will not work.
- Quality, consistency, and time are necessary to see meaningful results.
- Both social and traditional media can be relevant for many years.

Table 8. Social Media versus Traditional Marketing

Social Media Marketing	Traditional Marketing
Two-way communication: you can directly interact with clients and immediately get feedback about your services or ads.	One-way communication: clients receive information from consultants but are never able to communicate back.
Less control: any wrong information in your ad can result in very serious consequences since information travels quickly through the web. Also, users can post negative comments that everyone else will see.	More control: what you post in the ad is entirely up to you. You could make exaggerated claims since you control the entire message to target clients.
When brands create content, target clients expect discussion, comparison, and debate. Knowing this, it is not a good idea to broadcast claims about you (or your services) that isn't 100 percent true.	Target clients are constantly bombarded with claims like "best value" or "lowest price," thereby making it impossible for them to voice their opinion against these claims quickly or reasonably.

Continues.

70

Once target clients sense that you aren't being real, it's over. Trust is most important.	Target clients trust what you say about your brand.
Great tool to communicate what you are all about using personal branding as a competitive edge.	Cannot have back-and-forth contact with audience because ad is done using TV, radio, or print media.

DECIDING ON MARKETING THROUGH SOCIAL MEDIA?

Knowing now the limitations of social media, especially if you are advertising your services and wanting to get clients quickly—should you bother with social media? If you do, understand your audience and objective so you can decide whether social media will work for you. There is no perfect formula for social media marketing. Before you decide, do your research on what is your best option and select the one that will work for you.

MOST COMMON SOCIAL MEDIA TERMS

- **Adwords:** A popular Internet advertising program run by Google. Google generates revenue for paid searches on a "pay-per-click" basis, based on the number of clicks to searches of the keywords that you select.
- **Aggregator:** A website or software application that amasses information from multiple sources, for example: news sites, search engines, or social media.
- **Blog:** A web publishing tool that allows self-published posts, listed in reverse chronological order. Blog entries or posts are usually available as Really Simple Syndication (RSS) feeds, and frequently, but do not always, allow for commenting by readers. Popular blogging sites include Blogger, Wordpress, and Typepad.
- **Blogger:** A free blogging tool from Google, which can be linked to a Gmail account.
- **Blogosphere:** The sum of all blogs on the Internet and the conversations taking place within those blogs, including posts and comments.

- **Bookmarks/Bookmarking:** Saving an item, page, or website for future reference, increasingly via an online account such as Delicious (formerly del.icio.us). Works in a similar way to the "Favorites" feature of a web browser.
- **Chat:** Real-time interaction between two or more parties on a website or web application. Chat between two parties is also known as Instant Messaging.
- **Comment:** A response to a blog post, forum, or message board on behalf of a reader. Many blogs, but not all, allow for comments, and some require the blog owner to approve them before they are posted. Often, a blog will also provide an RSS feed for comments.
- **Communities:** Online networks that exist around shared interests or shared content.
- **Content Communities:** Communities that organize around and share particular kinds of content. Popular content communities exist around photos (Flickr), bookmarked links (Delicious), news (Digg), and videos (YouTube).
- **Connect:** The act of requesting admittance into an individual's network on LinkedIn.
- **Dashboard:** When referring to blogs, the administrative interface that allows users to post, upload files, etc. When referring to social media, an aggregator that allows users to simultaneously monitor activity on multiple social networks, including Facebook, Twitter, blogs, discussion forums, etc., or for multiple search terms on a single social network.
- **Facebook:** A social network where users maintain a profile of their personal interests, add friends, and exchange messages.
- **Follow:** The act of signing up on Twitter to send and see tweets.
- **Hyperlink:** A web reference that allows users to navigate from one document or page to another.
- **Instant Messaging (IM):** A form of real-time communication via the Internet between two or more people based on typed text, for example, Google Talk.
- **Keyword:** A subject or descriptive term that identifies the topic of a document, used to index documents for retrieval by search engines or other categorization. A keyword can appear in the

body of the text, subject heading, meta-data, etc., and is the basis for pay-per-click advertising.

- **LinkedIn:** A professional social networking tool where users maintain a profile of their professional expertise and accomplishments, connect with other users, join interest groups, post and search for jobs, and more. LinkedIn is the most "grown up" of the popular networks, which allows users to build their business and professional contacts into an online network.

- **Microblog:** Similar to a blog, although content is much more concise. The most well-known microblog is Twitter, which limits users to 140 characters.

- **Message boards:** Online discussion site where people can hold conversations in the form of posted messages.

- **MySpace:** A social network, similar to Facebook, where users maintain a profile of their personal interests, add friends, and exchange messages. Although MySpace is second in the market behind Facebook, it is known for having superior capabilities when it comes to music.

- **News Feed:** On Facebook, a live feed of status updates and wall posts, filtered by an algorithm which brings the items that are most relevant to each user to the top of the list.

- **Paid search:** Paid placement of a website in the search engine results for a particular keyword or keywords.

- **Pay-per-click:** A popular Internet advertising model, where the provider generates revenue only when a user clicks on the advertisement.

- **Profile:** An individual's identifying information requested when that individual signs up for a social networking site or other service. Profile information may include a username, contact information, personal or business interests, a photo, bio, or other data.

- **RSS:** A method of subscribing to a site's content and being alerted to new updates without visiting the site, either through the user's web browser or an RSS aggregator (for example, Bloglines).

- **RSS Feed:** A web standard that lets users subscribe to content from blogs, news stories, etc., through a feed reader, instead of by browsing from site to site.

- **Slidesharing:** A type of social network where users can upload, manage, and slide decks publicly or with their networks, and rate or comment on the slide decks of others. The most common example of slidesharing is SlideShare.
- **Tags/Tagging:** Keywords that label pieces of content (for instance, blog posts, bookmarks) and make them easy to organize and search.
- **Thread:** A strand of related messages that represent a conversation, e.g., messages on a discussion forum or a series of emails that use the same subject line, or a blog post and any related comments and trackbacks.
- **Twitter:** A popular microblogging tool, which allows users to share updates of no more than 140 characters, also known as tweets.
- **URL:** Stands for Uniform Resource Locator; the technical term for a Web address, e.g., http://www.ibm.com/us/en.sandbox/ver1/
- **Virtual Worlds:** An online environment in which people can interact with each other and the environment as 3D characters (avatars).
- **Vlogs:** Short clips of video; a blog that is comprised of video content or has video as well as text posts.
- **Wall:** On Facebook, a shared message board regarding an individual user that appears on the user's profile.
- **Web 2.0:** A term describing the generation of Web media such as blogs, social networks, etc., that emphasize self-publishing, collaboration, and interactive information sharing.
- **Wikis:** A website developed collaboratively by a community of users, allowing any user to add and edit content.

KEY POINTS

- Understand social media, its purpose, and its platforms.
- Understand social media marketing and the differences between social media and traditional marketing approaches. To have an effective marketing campaign, use a mix of social media and training marketing tools.

- Understand the advantages and disadvantages of each business-oriented social media site and select the best one to use to market your consulting services.
- Determine the marketing risks.
- Understand your role as a marketer and how to place ads in social media platforms.
- Define your target audience using selected social media advertising categories.
- Test out different creative ideas in advertising.
- Research and select the best option for you to use.
- Remember that social media is only one marketing strategy. It is best to mix your social media marketing with traditional marketing strategies.

Video marketing is a marketing option if you have the time, effort, and money to spend for your ads on TV and social media sites.

Chapter Six
Preparing a Business Plan

A plan keeps your effort going in the right direction. What's the use of running if you're not on the right road?
—**German proverb**

Whatever business you want to get into, a business plan is a "must" because it helps you decide whether consulting is the way to go, and a lending institution requires it if you borrow money to establish your business. You want to know where you are (your current state) so that you will know how to get there (your future state). Creating a business plan takes tremendous effort up front because you want to make sure you have everything in place. You cannot underestimate the importance of this roadmap, which shows the direction you plan to go.

BUSINESS PLAN DEFINED

A business plan is a written summary of what you hope to accomplish by being in business and how you intend to organize your resources to meet those goals. If a parallel may be drawn, a business plan is to a business executive what a blueprint is to a builder. A business plan describes who, what, when, where, why, how, and how much will make your business idea come to life. It is like an adventure story that should excite you and your readers (prospective clients and investors).

You will face many decisions during your first months of operation. You will make most of these decisions before you open your doors to the public. That's the best time to fully explore the alternatives, since you will not have daily business matters competing for your time, attention, and energy. Your business plan helps you anticipate these important decisions and give them the attention they deserve.

Ask yourself: How should I approach prospective clients? How much revenue do I need to generate to clear a profit? Can I make it by myself without a partner? If not, do I need a partner before I start? Your answers to these questions are critical if you want your consulting business to be successful. Your business plan helps you anticipate these important decisions because it performs three functions:

- The first and primary function is to force you to think through each aspect of your business. Most aspiring consultants think initially of their potential product and services and the market, but business has a wider scope.
- The second function is to allow you to have a "dry run," or a test, before you actually perform your first consulting engagement. Your business plan exposes you to potential sales, financing requirements, personnel, profits, and problems. It also simulates what you can expect in the early months and years of operation. A well-formulated business plan prepares you for the expected and frees your energy to handle the unexpected.
- The third function is as a sales tool that inspires confidence for both you and potential clients. If you become familiar with every aspect of your business, you will know what to expect and be self-confident.

A BUSINESS PLAN FOR A NEW BUSINESS

Since you are starting a new business as a consultant, your business plan will require developing a new set of assumptions, which will include costs, labor, pricing, and other factors. You should also identify essential events that must occur and actions to be taken, and a clear timetable to implement them (showing your activities in a chart).

Since you are just starting your consulting career, it would help you to tap into existing sources of information, for instance, from an industry group, association, or organization in your local area. Your marketing plan should be your most important document, which should explain your target audience and how you position your service to reach that audience. Your operational plan will explain how your business will be conducted daily.

A good business plan also includes a detailed account of your cash flow projections that set forth the projected timing of income and expenses. Most of these projections are tied directly to planned operational results.

PREPARING A BUSINESS PLAN

Planning and good management skills are vital to your business success. Those who do not prepare a plan run a very high risk of failure. Like the saying goes, "If you do not know where you are going in your personal or business life, there is little chance you will get to where you want to be."

FORMAT OF A BUSINESS PLAN

What goes into a business plan? Many things. Its content may vary depending on your consulting business and your clients. The trick is to write a business plan that meets every element of your clients' needs.

There are many business plan software packages available on the market. You will find business plan software in computer stores or you can buy one online. I examined *Business Plan Pro*, which has over 500 sample business costs. Currently, the standard edition costs $99 and a premier edition is $159.95. This software allows you to create a powerful business plan in seven steps, and it helps you through the entire process. It also gives you a full set of easy-to-understand financials with templates and spreadsheets to create text, tables, and charts using MS Word and Excel.

The *Business Plan Pro* software package is one of the best and can be a big help because the format and structure are already set up. All you need to do is enter your information. The advantage of using business plan software is that it saves time, but you shouldn't depend on using this tool alone. Check with business planners or people you know who have experience preparing business plans. A number of business plan software packages are available in the market today. Examples of the more popular packages include:

- *Business Plan Pro* by Palo Alto Software (www.businessplanpro. com).

- *Plan Write* by Business Resource Software (www.brs-inc.com)
- *Biz Plan Builder* by Jian Tools for Sales (www.jian.com).
- *Automate Your Business Plan* (www.business-plan.com)

WRITING A BUSINESS PLAN

You shouldn't go into consulting without putting your plan on paper. Writing a business plan is one of those hoops you must jump through, because it is not easy if you haven't done one before. Your plan must reflect your ultimate goal. It can accomplish many things for you and your business, but trying to make it be all things to all people is imprudent. One plan simply will not suffice for all possible uses. Sounds like a pain? It could be, but it does not have to be; it is not that difficult or time-consuming. Once you have done your homework and decide to go ahead, it does not take much effort to expand or adapt a business plan to your needs. *Table 9* gives you an outline of an informal business plan that I wrote for a client. *Table 10* is an example of a formal business plan outline that is usually used for longer and more complex projects.

Many years ago, I wrote a combined business/marketing plan for the purpose of setting up an executive communications exchange center for a large corporation. Although the process of putting a plan together should have been simple, at the time I didn't have sufficient experience preparing one, so it took a lot of time and iterations before I was comfortable finalizing it. In spite of receiving specific requirements from the client, I was not confident that the plan would ultimately meet his needs. Had I thought through the content carefully before just starting to write, and if I had clearly understood my client's needs, the process would have been simpler. Because I was unsure, my process for creating the plan became more complex and unwieldy than it needed to be.

KEEPING YOUR BUSINESS PLAN CURRENT

Once you have completed your business plan, do not just keep the document on file. Make sure to treat your plan as a dynamic document, keep it current as changes happen. If you don't keep your plan current, you will have to spend more time and effort when writing another plan. It's easier to edit an existing document than to start another one from scratch.

Table 9. Informal Business Plan Outline

The purpose of the project is to set up an Executive Communications Exchange Center (ECE) that top clients are invited to visit to get a tour of the facility. Very simply, it showcases different products offered by the client company.
Contents The plan consists of two phases. Phase I shows the conceptual overview that describes the future direction of an ECE. Phase II is the approach that describes the business plan and its processes.

Introduction

- Objective of the project.
- Background of the project, which is to sell outsourcing services and solutions.
- Methods to gather information.
- Background materials on outsourcing.
- Printed materials from the client.
- Personal interviews with other clients who are familiar with executive communications.
- Roundtable or group meetings with sales managers and their sales representatives.
- Surveys conducted with the client's headquarters managers.
- Best practices from selected external providers.
- Best practices from selected internal providers.
- These sources provide a combination of fact and opinion, both of which are important in developing a conceptual framework. Generalizations will be made in some instances in order to apply them to the abstract concept. This plan shows the result of the synthesis of the ideas gathered brought together in a basic structure and design.

Organization of the report

- Phase I: Project Overview. This section briefly describes the what, why, and who aspects of the project.
- Phase II: Project Approach.
- Business plan. This plan looks at the business planning aspects, including the vision of the company, purpose, objectives, and strategies of the project.
- Processes. The processes section looks at some general tactics and activities needed to successfully launch and run the project. External tactics are positioning, promotion/advertising medium, packaging, and showcasing. Internal tactics are pilot testing, benchmarking for best practices, communication process, measurements, and the engagement plan.

> - Phase III: Project Content. This is the development plan required to imple-ment an ECE, which includes the actual core information presented to pro-spective clients.
> - Conclusion.
>
> **Appendices**
> - Client visit process flowchart.
> - Project implementation timeline.
> - Input from various sources with similar projects.

Table 10. Formal Business Plan Outline

Cover page (the title and date of your plan)
The cover sheet contains all the usual and appropriate identification information about your business.
This includes the name, address, and telephone number of the business and the names, addresses, and phone numbers of all owners or corporate officers (or if you are a sole proprietor, your information). On this sheet you should also tell who prepared the business plan and when prepared or revised. (In most cases, you can ask the assistance of a business or financial planner, if you have not yet had experience creating a business plan.) To help you keep track of copies you send to lenders and prospective clients, include a place for marking each cover sheet with a copy number.
Table of contents (a list of the contents of your plan with page numbers)
The table of contents should clearly and simply lead the reader to each of the docu-ments in your plan.
Having a table of contents helps the reader move smoothly from one section of your plan to another when verifying information. For example, if a lender is reading financial information regarding advertising on a pro forma cash flow statement, he or she can use the table of contents to locate the section for specifics about where you will be advertising and how the advertising money will be spent. The table of contents also refers to the page in the supporting documents section that contains advertising rate sheets backing up the advertising plan.
Statement of purpose (or executive summary)
The executive summary is the most important part of your document, because it provides an overview of the entire plan.
Your statement of purpose summarizes your plan and states your objectives. If you are seeking loan funds or investment capital, your statement of purpose will list your

capital needs, how you intend to use the money, the benefit of the loan funds to your business, and how you intend to repay the loan or return profits to the investor.

While you are writing your plan, many of your early ideas will change and new ideas develop that's appropriate and for that reason, the statement of purpose is most effectively formulated after writing your plan. This statement should be concise—no longer than one page.

Plan I: Organizational Plan (the first main section of your business plan)
This section contains information on how your business is put together administratively. It includes such things as a description of your business, your legal structure, who your management and personnel will be, where you will be located if your location is not tied to your marketing, how you will do your accounting, what insurance you will have, and what security measures you will take to protect inventory and information.

Plan II: Marketing Plan (the second main section of your business plan)
Your marketing plan contains information on your total market with emphasis on your target market. Include information on your target market and your competition, and the decisions you are making for the promotion of your product or services, pricing, timing of market entry, and where to locate if that is tied into your marketing. You also examine current industry trends.

Plan III: Financial Documents (the third major section of your business plan)
Your financial documents translate the information in the first two sections of your plan into financial figures that can be used to analyze your business and make decisions for higher profitability.

Plan IV: Supporting documents (documents referred to and used to back up statements made in the three main sections of your business plan)
This section includes: owner/manager résumés, personal financial statements, articles of incorporation/partnership agreements, legal contracts, lease agreements, proprietary assets (copyrights, trademarks, and patents), letters of reference, demographics, and any other documents that are pertinent to supporting the plan.

Appendix
The Appendix is the repository for those items that aren't part of the business plan itself but are helpful to someone reading the plan.

Also include your marketing materials (brochures, ads) in the Appendix. If you are just starting out, you might consider including résumés of key employees if you will be using others to supplement your skill and experience.

Business plan writing services. There are a number of business plan writing services available that you can tap into but it would be beneficial if you try putting together your first draft. By going through the process yourself, even if you're not a good writer, you'll be forced to think through how you can market your services.

If you are still unsure about writing your business plan yourself, you can find plenty of low- or no-cost resources such as the following:

Local Small Business Development Center. It can provide free and confidential counseling with assistance and review of your draft business plan, as well as many other free counseling services. Visit www.asbdc-us.org for the center nearest you.

SCORE (Service Corps for Retired Executives). Partner of the SBA and boasts 370 chapters nationwide consisting of retired and working volunteers, entrepreneurs and corporate managers/executives. SCORE helps you build your own business, provides current resources and connects you with business professionals who can share knowledge and provide advice at no charge. To contact SCORE, call 1-800-634-0245, email contactus@score.org or visit their website at www.score.org.

Your local college. If you can offer a meaty assignment, you might be able to attract a business student to help you write your business plan. If not, see if the college has a business college club that can help.

Trade association. All professions have trade associations that can help you refine your business plan ideas. Visit the association's website or call them for help.

KEY POINTS

- Create a business plan describing the who, what, when, where, how, and how much relating to your business.
- Prepare a business plan using templates and business plan software. If you have no prior experience, engage the services of a financial planner or check out business plan writing services.
- Be prepared to face many difficult decisions during the first few months of start-up.
- Seek recommendations to help with business plan creation.
- Customize your business plan according to client needs. Do not use a boilerplate because every need is unique. Each plan should meet every element of the client's needs.
- Keep your business plan current so you don't start from scratch the next time you need to write another plan.

Chapter Seven
Obtaining Financing

High finance isn't burglary or obtaining money by false pretenses, but rather a judicious selection from the best features of those fine cuts.
—**Finley Peter Dunne**

Obtaining financing may be one of the most difficult tasks you face, because without seed money you cannot start, whether that money comes from your own savings or from loans. Borrowing money is risky when you have no cash reserves in the bank. Ask yourself what you will do if you do not survive your first year in the business. How will you pay interest on the loan you are borrowing? Are you willing to take the risk? Are there people you can count on for support in case you fail? There is no easy or simple answer to these questions.

SEED MONEY

How much money will you need to survive during your first year in business? To begin, estimate in very round—perhaps unrealistically high—figures.

Example 1. When you calculate how much money you may need to get started, put down on paper, say, $31,000 (rounded up from 30,500). Rounding keeps things in perspective and reminds you that the numbers you calculate do not have a direct impact on your first year of consulting.

Why not? Because at this point you are still reviewing your financial needs and income level. The numbers you create are only estimates. You will see a clearer picture once you review your numbers with your banker, loan officer, or financial advisor. It is helpful to also go over things with an accountant.

Example 2. Let's say your consulting business has monthly expenses of exactly $5,000 for the first year. It is January and you have just begun your enterprise. We know that within this month, you are going to spend $5,000. How much income are you going to take in? More than likely, zero. Remember that in the first month, you will be doing a lot of things: marketing, strategizing, meeting people. Actually making substantial revenue from these jobs is probably not going to happen right away.

Once you complete your business plan and financial projections, you should have a clearer idea of your short-term and medium-term financial needs. You will want to be familiar with the types of financing available, the various sources, the ways to approach banks or other financial institutions, and the types of guarantee(s) that may be required of you.

TYPES OF FINANCING

1.EQUITY FINANCING

The money you put into a business is equity. Equity financing means money you borrow from the cash value of your property or money from other investors. This sounds simple but may not always be possible to obtain. You are limited to raising the money yourself through your available savings, selling or mortgaging your house (if you own one), or calling on family and friends for help. If you reach a point where you need to raise equity capital, seek the advice of financial experts; you may have to prepare a more detailed business plan.

2.DEBT FINANCING

You can borrow from banks, savings and loans, insurance companies, the government (SBA), and other financial institutions. The SBA has an extensive list of publications that provide information about financing sources and available programs. You can also borrow from family and friends, but wherever you seek a loan, you must repay it with interest.

With borrowed money, normally the principal and interest are paid monthly. You need to take into account the repayment of principal and interest as expenses in your current business plan.

TYPES OF SECURITY LENDERS REQUIRE

Again, you have to consult your lender because there are so many types of security that you can get, depending on your current financial situation. You could use an endorser, guarantor, co-maker, or promissory note. You need to provide whatever your lender asks for.

Using a personal guarantor might be risky. Acceptable personal guarantees must be backed up with assets that the bank can seize upon default, such as a house, car, personal bank accounts, investments, wages from an employer, and so on.

If you decide to borrow, you need to know how the process works. When you are new at obtaining financing, before applying for a loan, check with your financial advisor or talk to a loan officer at a bank or financial institution to get the specifics.

KEY POINTS

- Use seed money to get your consulting business started. It is difficult to gauge how much you will need because every business is different and factors that come into play also vary. The best way to plan your needs is to start with round numbers, which are only estimates based on your business plan and financial projections.
- Finance your consulting business by raising the money yourself or by borrowing from the bank, other financial institutions, or friends and family.
- Be prepared to provide security, which is often required by the lender if you do not have sufficient collateral, depending on your current financial situation. Security can be an endorser, guarantor, co-maker, or promissory note.

Chapter Eight
Marketing Your Consulting Services

A man's success in business today depends upon his power of getting people to believe he has something they want.
—**Gerald Stanley Lee**

Marketing creates an awareness of and demand for your services; both are essential for success in the consulting business. The marketing process involves many steps that will lead to convincing potential clients that their needs can be met and their problems solved by your specific services.

Develop a mission statement that defines who you are and where you are going in your consultancy practice; this will clearly define your abilities to yourself and your clients.

MARKETING PLAN DEFINED

A marketing plan is like a roadmap: it guides you toward specifically stated goals and objectives. Once you develop a mission statement (what you believe in and the things you will do to implement that belief) for your business, you will be able to set more specific goals and objectives. Next, decide on the means to your end; that is, the specific marketing tactics that can help you meet your stated goals.

Tailor your marketing plan to your goals and objectives. This plan is a starting point—a place from which to begin your course of action. If you don't know how to create a marketing plan, many books are available to guide you in preparing one or you can seek answers from someone with marketing experience.

MARKETING TECHNIQUES

The marketing techniques you plan to use will vary, depending on what best meets your needs. You use marketing techniques or devices for several purposes; your main purpose is to obtain new clients and establish a client base, especially if you are just starting your consulting business.

After you decide how you want to market, you must focus your message on the key points that you want to communicate. Whatever your plan is, ask yourself what messages will attract prospective clients.

Once you make a decision about what and why you want to market, choose the most appropriate marketing tool that will be cost-effective for you. Use a tool or tools to clearly send your message.

My consultant friends tell me that they started with word-of-mouth referrals (most effective marketing tools) from trusted sources. They actually generated more business through word-of-mouth than through advertising.

Let's start with word-of-mouth referrals and technological tools like the web, followed by more traditional approaches.

WORD-OF-MOUTH REFERRALS

This is the most potent form of marketing since relationship marketing has a huge impact. If someone knows you and is aware of your abilities, you have an opportunity to ask for referrals. The easiest referrals for a newcomer who has no client history is to belong to professional organizations or associations.

Always ask permission to use the referring person's name. A referral doesn't necessarily result in an immediate contract, although that's certainly a possibility. Acting on a referral is for potential business. Never pressure prospective clients; simply inform them that their associate (referral's name) suggested you give them a call. Say that you worked with that associate in some successful program that provided a real benefit for both of you.

Keep the call cordial, professional, and low key. Follow the call with a very brief letter (the brevity shows that you understand how valuable time is), summarizing the same points you outlined in your call. Mention that you look forward to speaking again sometime in the future, then check in by telephone or email every few weeks and see what happens.

If you are a member of a networking group or are active in associations and local organizations, you may be able to get consulting assignments through referrals from fellow members and associates. Those fellow members and associates might also give you leads to companies and people who are looking for consultants for short-term projects. Getting referrals through your networking group really works; I have gotten several consulting projects through networking. Each was a short-term project but it paid well and allowed me the flexibility of working from home.

The best referrals—after you establish your name—are those that lead to clients calling *you*.

ONLINE MARKETING

Online marketing includes the use of websites and email to forward your advertising messages to prospective clients.

WEBSITES

In today's world, you cannot pick up a newspaper or magazine or even watch TV without being reminded about the Internet. The World Wide Web is everywhere; all local and global organizations use the web every day to see what's new and what products and services can be purchased online. People who are responsible for setting up and maintaining web pages use it more often than ordinary users. As part of dramatic changes in the way you communicate to people you do business or share information with, the web has become very popular.

The World Wide Web has great potential as a consulting-marketing medium. You can build your own website and load a lot of your information onto the Internet. You can write a newsletter that will be accessible to anyone—anywhere and everywhere. The Internet is a low-cost tool to get people to look at services you offer.

If you build your own website, keep your content current, ensure that the content appeals to your target audience, be consistent with your message, and ensure that it is user-friendly and easy to navigate.

PRINT MATERIALS

Use print materials to communicate your services to potential clients. An example could be creating and publishing your own newsletter to market your services and proactively search for clients. Newsletters allow you to reach out to prospective clients and keep existing clients informed, and they are a particularly effective way to generate favorable publicity and build your client base. Other physical marketing tools include stationery and business cards.

Prospective clients want specific information they can use, and a newsletter is an effective way to showcase you as a reliable source of such information. You can distribute your newsletters by email as well as in print to hand out to friends and colleagues who can pass them around to others.

E-ZINE ADVERTISING

Advertise your services in e-magazines to reach target markets for a modest cost, but before you do, know the basics, statistics for circulation, demographics, and e-magazine's policies.

E-NEWSLETTERS

E-newsletters are a great marketing tool to use to get potential clients. Before you create one, check out Ralph Wilson's e-zine *Web Marketing Today* (www.wilsonweb.com).

DIRECT MAIL

Pieces that you mail directly to targeted clients can be very effective. Brochures, letters, flyers, and other forms of physical mail can be used as direct-mail pieces. Brochures are used most often as a back-up tool. Brochures are to be left with prospects after your first exploratory meeting or mailed to them when they first inquire about your services.

ONLINE SOCIAL NETWORKING

Use online social networking on social media sites such as LinkedIn. com. You can post topics on threads that deal with your area of expertise and you can respond to others' postings to establish a reputation as an expert. Make sure that you do not use too may of these social media sites or else you will spread yourself too thin.

COMMUNITY RELATIONS

Community relations play an important role in your marketing program. By participating in community events, you can increase your exposure in your neighborhood. Meet with community leaders and support community efforts, such as posting signage about upcoming events.

NETWORK MARKETING

Network marketing involves interacting one-on-one with potential clients. This activity involves seeking out and meeting others in your business community. Through networking, you will gain an opportunity to ask for referrals.

SPEECHES, SEMINARS, AND WORKSHOPS

Presentations at corporate meetings/events, industry conferences, or public seminars can be extremely effective publicity generators. Many financial or training consultants conduct their own public seminars or align themselves with the adult educational services of colleges and universities in their areas. If you don't already have an extensive list of prospects for publicizing your seminar, you can rent mailing lists for any profession and any zip code from a list broker. Trainers who have written their own books have the opportunity to showcase their books to participants. A perfect example is my one-time mentor, Rob L. Jolles, an established author of several books about sales training and conducting presentations and meetings. He has the advantage of showing his books and talking about them with his participants, because he is a trainer by profession. Presentations are an effective approach for him.

COLD SALES CALLS

This process is a must for newcomers. There are consultants who find most of their clients by making personal calls on prospects—almost literally knocking on doors and making sales presentations directly and in person. However, not all of these sales calls are totally cold (via telephone, email, or making a connection on social network); few consultants contact prospective clients without being asked to first. If you call without any invitation, this method can be difficult for you since it is time-consuming and may not have a high rate of return. A better approach is to send letters or brochures first; then there is a good chance that some recipients will follow up with a phone call and ask for you to see them in person.

> Before I invite consultants to make their presentations to me, I check the types of consulting services they offer. I want to make sure they are not wasting their time and mine if their services do not meet my needs. I usually ask them to send me their brochures first so I can see their products and services. Because these contacts are cold sales calls, I ask for references of companies or people in those companies who have used their services before. If I'm interested, I might call and check those references.

ASSOCIATIONS AND SOCIETIES

You can join the right association or society to network with members and generate potential clients not just through members, but also through their referrals. This venue allows you to meet people and tell them about what you can do. Some associations and societies you can get involved in are The Chamber of Commerce business associations (a bedrock of local networking), service clubs, referral groups, the Toastmasters International Club. The International Society of Performance Improvement (ISPI) and the American Society for Training and Development (ASTD) are good for people in the training field.

You can benefit from any reputable groups that could provide you with an opportunity to socialize with its members. If any of the groups are tied in somehow to the business you're establishing, join it. Shake hands with people; find out who does what, tell them what you do! Remember the point here is not to just meet people, but to build a client base. Be prepared to enter the group with an objective: to pass the word along, give your name, business location, and the fact that you offer consulting services to people who need help in your area of expertise. Make sure that the business card you circulate reinforces the specifics, and you're ready to roll. I joined Toastmasters International in early 1999 to enhance my presentation skills. Before joining, I already had experience doing presentations, but I was not comfortable speaking in front of a large audience. I was always anxious in case I could not answer all the questions posed to me. I don't have those jitters now; the practice I got by being a member was invaluable. Being able to comfortably present in front of people is useful if you are a consultant, but the most client-productive associations to join are those that your target niche focuses on to improve *their* skills and further *their* careers. Volunteer to serve on committees to prove your worth. (My editor friend, for example, belongs to two associations of writers in a specific niche plus two associations of small publishers—her precise markets.)

MASS MEDIA ADVERTISING

The various media—in newspapers, magazines, radio, TV, and now the Internet—have an insatiable appetite for interviewing interesting, informative, and entertaining people. You can either approach the media directly with story ideas or hire someone to make the arrangements for you. Several sources publish blurbs about experts in their field who are available for media interviews. For a few hundred dollars a year you have unlimited exposure to all sorts of media.

General advertising carries with it certain problems that you should be aware of. Building your client base is the name of the game in your first year of consulting practice, but paid advertising is a poor way to do it. Why? It is not cost-effective. If you want to advertise, select a specialized publication.

Part of the cost of advertising is the amount of time it takes you to get a response that develops into a job. Industry pros say you need a minimum of nine exposures. That cost of this can be very high. If you decide that you must advertise, do your best to advertise cost-effectively. If you are from the Washington, D.C., metropolitan area, use a well-known periodical that has wide readership, such as *The Washington Post*, or advertise in the newsletters of the organizations your target prospects belong to—which you have just joined.

YOUR OWN WEBSITE

Other than the various media sources above, you might explore creating your own website for marketing and professional image purposes. If you are an experienced web designer, you can create it yourself; if you are not, seek someone who can design it for you, at a minimal cost. If you plan to create your own website, think about the nature of your medium and your target audience. What should you include on your website? Essential information such as details of your consulting service, informational articles, a frequently-asked questions section related to your field of consulting, partial list of your clients, and some client testimonials.

Guidelines for your web page: Keep it short; use color; include a short list of your top attractions; keep your headlines short (ten items or less); explain (not just describe) your services using active voice/phrases; use large and attractive pictures and images to make them stand out; make sure your logo is big, bold, and colorful to make it stand out; use simple typefaces (limit to three to four typefaces in a single page); use contrast(never use all caps in the body text, but it's okay to use in headlines); use white space (don't crowd every inch of space with text); submit your website to search engines because people use the Internet for searching any and all types of information. You can hire a specialist to do your optimization by picking out the keywords and descriptions and submitting your website to various search engines (such as Google and Yahoo).

ARTICLES AND BOOKS

Writing articles and books in your area of expertise is one of the best ways to build your credibility and get name recognition. As a freelance magazine and newspaper writer and a published book author myself, editors who have worked with me tell me what's hot to write about, or they suggest I write about subjects I am an expert on. Readers are particularly hungry for articles written from an insider's perspective.

As an independent consultant, you may want to write articles about problems you have solved for others. Disguise the names and use experiences from your employment days as you would have resolved them had you been an outsider.

If you are a contributing writer, the publication(s) you write for may not pay you for your efforts, but you reap the benefits of free publicity and establish a name for yourself as an expert. Some may offer you free ad space. Just make sure that the publications you write for have a large readership among your target prospects. Likewise, writing a book can make you an instant expert in the eyes of the media and your prospects. You also gain interviews more easily and enjoy other opportunities to get your word out.

I started being a freelance newspaper and magazine writer in 1997. I got paid on a fee basis as a contributing writer for a local newspaper; one magazine gave me free publicity only. As a beginner, it didn't perturb me, since I needed the exposure.

INDUSTRY LEADS

Your current industry contacts are potentially the richest source of leads for your consulting practice. These are the people who already know you and what you can do. Keeping in touch with your contacts is essential. You want your name to be first on their minds if they have a consulting opportunity or can refer one to you.

> Suzanne, a good friend and an independent consultant told me that when she started her consulting practice, her first letter was a dud. She had written a four-page letter to introduce herself. She counted 20 "I's" in that first letter. When she showed the letter to a consulting firm, she was told, "You talk as if you are very formal and that you're totally concentrating on yourself as opposed on the other person. They're not interested in you, they're interested in themselves." Suzanne learned quickly from the feedback.

In addition to marketing techniques and tools, you have to think about shaping prospective clients' perceptions of you and your product or services through *positioning*. Simply, this means creating a place or niche in the marketplace for you and your product or services. *See Exercise 4: Choosing Appropriate Marketing Techniques.*

In positioning, consider these basic elements and choices:

PRICE

You can go high or low, or even average, depending on your overall marketing strategy and business philosophy. Your price may depend on your experience. Obviously, you cannot charge a very high price if you are just starting. It is advisable to create your list of consulting services with your price range. This way, depending on the type and complexity of the project, you are able to charge the appropriate fees without either overpricing the client or under pricing your services.

QUALITY

In the minds of many potential clients, price and quality are directly linked. If you price low, you will attract initial jobs that get you started, but you will have an uphill battle establishing a perception of quality. It is difficult to separate the two. This is where your research helps; ask other independent consultants who provide the same service as you to get their insight.

EXCLUSIVITY

This is a contract term where a client grants a consultant sole rights to a particular project. Like quality, this is linked to price. You want to ensure that your qualifications and experiences are commensurate with the price you are asking.

POPULARITY

This is the opposite of exclusivity. Some business prospects go where the crowd goes, but popularity is normally associated with low price; it is hard to separate the two.

Many, if not most, consultants are in almost desperate need of help in their marketing strategy and winning the kind of clients they want. Failures in marketing are responsible for many failed consulting practices. Attracting quality prospects is rarely the easiest thing to do but it is probably the most critical factor.

LOOK LIKE A PRO

You must have heard the saying: "Is image everything?" Absolutely! Image is important to everyone who aspires to influence others in any way. In your marketing and consulting work generally, your image translates into a confidence factor, helping to lend credibility to you as a consultant as well as to your specific claims and promises. Develop your personal presence, which includes how you dress, how you conduct yourself, how you use your voice, and how you present yourself in meetings. Keep in mind that other people are generally more comfortable with people who are like them. You should dress and conduct yourself accordingly.

HOW A CLIENT CHOOSES A CONSULTANT

Today, clients choose a consultant because of his or her perceived value to their company. In earlier years—the 1970s and 1980s in particular—consultants were hired for other reasons. In the seventies, companies looked for consultants who could motivate their employees. In the eighties, companies looked for consultants who had higher education, because they expected them to solve problems.

In the nineties, the roles of consultants evolved, so that now, in the 21st century, companies are searching for much more: good ideas, innovative solutions, strategic thinking, effective planning, and successful implementation. Demand is becoming more sophisticated as companies become more sophisticated. As a new consultant, you will do much better if you are a specialist rather than a generalist.

> Suzanne's experience has been 100 percent word-of-mouth referrals, which she knows is not typical. She learned the value of not "burning your bridges" because you never know when you might need a good word from a former client.

HOW TO SELL YOURSELF

Remember that consultants are hired for specific projects and for specific periods, with no guarantees. As a result, potential clients have no qualms whatsoever about firing you if your project is not working out as planned, if the company's strategy changes unexpectedly, or if—for some reason—the project runs out of funding.

Exercise 4
Choosing Appropriate Marketing Techniques

Here is a list of most common marketing techniques you can use. The advantages and disadvantages of each that are discussed above are also summarized below. Rank the methods you are most likely to use based on your money and time. In the fourth column, rank your answers starting from 1 (most advantageous) through 10 (least advantageous). This exercise will help you set your priorities for your business plan.

1 Technique	2 Advantages	3 Disadvantages	4 Your Ranking
Word-of-mouth	Referral from an associate	Time-consuming	
Email	Low-cost means to reach decision-makers	Needs email access and a large prospect list	
Newsletter	An effective way to build clientele	Must write well or hire someone to write for you	
Speeches, seminars, and workshops	Extremely effective public-ity and credibility genera-tor	Needs public speaking or training skills	
Brochures	Handy tool after first meeting with prospect	Less effective for making initial contact	
Cold sales calls	Personal contact with prospects	Time-consuming if you approach the client uninvited	
Organizations or associations	Allow you to meet people, tell them what you can do, and show them your skills by volunteering	Expensive and time-consuming until you find the right organizations	
Direct mail	Useful if part of a multi-pronged campaign	Expensive, if the 1% to 10% response rate is to pay off	
Advertising	Useful if combined with other techniques; it can be very costly. Poor tool for a beginning consultant		
Articles and books	Great way to build cred-ibility and name recogni-tion	Need writing skills and experience	
Industry leads	Current contacts are the richest source	Limited opportunity until you build industry contacts	
Directories and lists	Identify vendors' directo-ries in which to be listed	Supplemental tool to be combined with other media	

FINDING OR DEFINING YOUR NICHE

The consulting business covers very broad areas in which you can specialize, play different roles, and use different approaches in marketing your skills.

You have to find or define your niche, however, because you cannot be all things to all people. You should be viewed as an expert in specific areas. Focus more on areas that you do best. Besides, being a jack-of-all-trades is inviting disaster. You are spreading yourself too thin and the quality of your services will eventually suffer. Remember, your intent is to keep your existing clients and continue to add to your client base. Word-of-mouth from even one dissatisfied client travels fast. Getting blacklisted will seriously affect your chances for success in the consulting business, so put a lot of thought into your specialization.

Here is a quick summary of the various skill sets of people who can realistically expect, with hard work, to make a success of themselves in the consulting field. If you're not on this list, it does not mean you can't be a consultant. It means only that you should take a good look at your skills, background, and expertise, and come up with a solid "package" that clients will view as a realistic option for resolving tangible business problems.

Other than your specialization, your credentials could include publications, awards, and other achievements in your field. These help you establish special credentials for special projects in which you must compete with other consultants for a given contract.

With the avalanche of downsizing that occurred in the 1990s and so far in the 21st century, companies have become more lean and mean. Employees are often handling more than one job; most of the time, they cannot do all the tasks themselves. Companies hire consultants to fill the void. Many functions, especially in the service areas such as training, marketing, and human resources, have been devastated by these cutbacks.

Consultants are hired to perform the functions of employees who are no longer around. Specialists in virtually every consulting field are in demand and ten areas in particular are the "hottest." These fields are booming, and this is good news.

The bad news is that consulting is not what it used to be. A new breed of consultants is focused on taking advantage of the impact made by the dramatic downsizing trends. And to add to the number of people getting into consulting are the retirees (the baby boomers) who are still interested in working. If you are a retiree and the company you worked for is interested in hiring you back as a consultant, this is a great opportunity to start your career as a consultant. You have the advantage of already knowing the job, the people you worked with, the systems, and the company policies and procedures. You are not considered an outsider because you already had your foot in the door.

COVETED CONSULTANT SKILLS

What kinds of skills do you need to be a consultant? You need to be:

ANALYTICAL

One of the things you do is analyze available data to figure out appropriate solutions to problems. You need the ability to discern the root causes of your clients' problems.

A GOOD LISTENER

Listen to your clients and be clear when answering their questions. Most often, people tend to think about what they will say next rather than listen to what their clients are saying. Consulting is about communicating and good listening skills help you do a better job. When you are talking to your clients and they see that you are focused on what they are telling you, you show respect and make them feel important. To be an active listener, ask open-ended questions that help define the big picture, the boundaries of your opportunities, and your solutions. Ask questions and make sure you are understood so you know exactly what each client wants from you.

A NEGOTIATOR

Master the art of negotiating to get and keep clients. A good negotiator understands how to build and sustain a consultant-client relationship, how to identify what clients need, give them what they need, and get what they want in return.

A PROBLEM SOLVER

In consulting, "problem-solving is where the rubber meets the road." You have to review the data you gather, "peeling the onion" as much as you can so you get to the root causes. This is where your research skills will play a part. Problem solving entails brainstorming for ideas, then eliminating the poor ones and keeping the good ones. Weigh all possible alternatives until you are convinced you have the best possible course of action.

A STRATEGIC THINKER

Strategic thinking is coming up with innovative solutions to complex problems. For strategic thinking to occur, you have to integrate several types of mental skills and techniques, habits, and attitudes in the context of defining the client's problem. Because you have to be open-minded, you cannot use a "cookbook" approach. You have to be able to generate new (but useful) ideas for overcoming routine ways of doing your work, and of putting together information.

Table 11. Clients' Wants

Accomplishment	Guts	Skills
Authenticity	Information	Style
Approval	Insight	Support
Compassion	Objectivity	Time
Credibility	Personality	Values
Experience	Perspective	Vision
Expertise	Products	Wisdom
Friendship	Reputation	

CHANGES IN YOUR LIFESTYLE

The lifestyles of most consultants differ from those of average business people. Consulting is envisioned as a lavish industry: exorbitant fees, first-class travel, and hobnobbing with top executives. This image presents only the positive side for those highly successful professionals.

Let's look at the more realistic side of the business:

- Working hours: Most consultants set their own hours, based on their biological clocks. If you're a morning person, you tend to start early. If you're an evening person, you tend to start in the afternoon and work through the night. Whatever time you start, the working hours are long. You may have to sacrifice your weekends when deadlines are tight.

- Amount of effort needed: When you are working on problems that are complicated or need strategic planning and thinking, you get absorbed in the project. You may spend several days on it until the situation is resolved. This effort becomes especially draining if you are working on concurrent projects.
- Working relationships: Consulting is a people-business, so you need to know how to work with others. Even if you have the technical, managerial, and administrative skills that got you hired, a lack of people skills will impede your working smoothly with your clients; all your brilliant ideas will not come to naught if you have difficulty working and communicating with people at all levels.

WHAT YOU NEED TO MARKET YOUR SERVICES

Once you've made the decision that you want to be a consultant, ask yourself:

- **What has to be present for me to be satisfied with my consulting practice?**
  To become a successful independent consultant, you need a certain level of professional expertise in a niche market. Other than subject matter expertise, your kind of consulting might require certification and licensing (financial advisor, for instance). Plan and organize before you start your career as a consultant.
- **Is consulting my only source of income?**
  If so, this weighs very heavily on your decision to be a consultant. If you're supporting a family, they can get really nervous when that paycheck disappears. The only way to solve this issue is to continually look for work opportunities. You must be confident in the value of what you have to offer, possess the materials and skills to help you put your best foot forward, and be able to live with uncertainty and ambiguity.
- **What must happen for me to know that I'm satisfied with my choice of career?**
  Other than professional and financial considerations, you have to think about your family and friends. Are they supportive of your decision to become a consultant, especially if they know you already have a good-paying job? Can you work without the

daily social interaction that you are used to? Working for yourself versus working for a company also changes your lifestyle completely. As an independent consultant, you have to motivate yourself and be self-disciplined. In the beginning, you may have to cut back on expenses such as eating out, traveling for pleasure, and taking time for your family and friends.

CONSULTING SPECIALTY VERSUS YOUR MARKETING NEEDS

Individuals who have a broad consulting expertise are able to change their specialty according to current market opportunities. This is now common among independent consultants who have the flexibility to create several résumés to match each opportunity. For instance, some multitalented individuals have as much as a dozen résumés, each of which focuses on a different kind of experience and capability. In my case, when I apply for a technical writer position, I customize my résumé to match the requirements of that position. Some clients seeking technical writers like me require that applicants be familiar with some given specification of equipment. For example, I saw a job vacancy for a technical writer position to support a Department of Defense client; this job required knowledge of HM&E (Hull Mechanical and Electrical Equipment), so I accented this skill in my résumé since I was familiar with it.

CONSULTANT DEGREE OF SPECIALIZATION

A consultant can specialize in various areas. In my own case, I tend to accept consulting work in the field of instructional design and development rather than technical writing and editing because several of the consulting projects that came my way in the past few years were focused on designing and developing training programs. I accepted these types of projects because the opportunities were there. Other than opportunity, my choice was also based on personal judgment and objectives. Although I have been working as a technical writer for years, I didn't want to lose my skills in designing training programs.

Normally, when you are new to consulting, you start at some position and make adjustments as you realize what works and what doesn't. Keep an open mind; be prepared to learn and adapt, be flexible. I learned from experience that no matter what your specialty as a consultant is, you should be alert to other specialties within your consulting framework.

WINNING CLIENTS

In addition to producing an effective marketing strategy, find other ways to win clients. One way to appeal to potential clients is to be a specialist (rather than a generalist). Another way is to stress your achievements, much more than your years of experience. These achievements are powerful credentials that are important to whoever you are marketing to. For example, being a manager and director of marketing is not nearly as important as having written proposals that won millions for a former employer.

RESOLVING CLIENT PROBLEMS

Even when you are working closely with a key person in the client organization, it is common to run into a conflict or a problem. There will always be one or more people (if there is a program team) who resist your help or advice, regard your presence as an intrusion in their company, or resent your seemingly high, hourly gross income.

Whether the assignment should be ended or not depends on the seriousness of the problem and the status of the key client. You have to analyze who you are having problems with, why, and what problems need to be resolved if you are to continue working on the project per your contract. This may be tough for a new consultant who hasn't learned the ropes or faced a similar problem before. Resolving issues without undue pain and hardship could be the luck of the draw. Sometimes it's a personality clash. Problems and conflicts happen often. No matter what approach you use, if you are unable to recognize or prevent a problem before it grows, your only option is to bow out gracefully. This might involve losing unbilled hours, but sometimes that's the way consulting goes. You need to protect your reputation as a professional.

KEY POINTS

- Create a marketing plan to guide you in achieving your business goals.
- Sell yourself by using the most appropriate marketing techniques, which could be a combination of, say, word-of-mouth referrals and industry leads. If the techniques you select are not effective, try others. Depending on your situation, you have the flexibility to make changes.

- Position yourself well by considering basic elements of price, quality, exclusivity, and popularity.
- Review your consulting skills against those commonly referenced, which include, among others, being a good listener, analyst, problem-solver, and strategist.
- Deepen your areas of specialization and think about being a specialist rather than a generalist. More and more industry-based companies look for specializations in areas like healthcare, finance, telecommunications, or information technology.
- Examine the hottest consulting practices and see where you fit or how you can improve yourself to take advantage of what's in demand.
- Review consulting trends to give you insight on the direction of consulting.
- Investigate newer online marketing options (such as social media) that can help you reach prospective clients.
- Familiarize yourself with the laws governing electronic marketing by visiting the FTC website or contacting your industry association before you start using these electronic marketing tools. Market online using Search Engine Optimization (SEO), pay per click (PPC), emails, and blogging.

Chapter Nine
Exploring the Internet and Integrating Information into Your Marketing Techniques

Technologies emerging today will give us the ability to explore, convey, and create knowledge as never before . . . I believe that if we respond with our best creative energies, we can unleash a new renaissance of discovery and learning.
—**John Scully, former CEO at Apple Inc.**

The Internet is a powerful electronic tool that you can use to obtain information and marketing venues. As a new consultant, you can subscribe for free to *Web Digest* at www.wdfin.com. WDFN is a weekly email newsletter that delivers short reviews of marketing-oriented websites. Topics include direct marketing, search engine marketing, email marketing, and many more.

WHY THE INTERNET?
The Internet opens a world of opportunities. In our competitive marketplace, you can advertise your products and services online. It used to be that traditional approaches, such as paper-based advertising through ads in newspapers and magazines, brochures and pamphlets, direct mail, and letters were most effective. Today, the rules have changed radically. Now, you are remiss if you don't have access to the web or, preferably, have your own website.

In an earlier chapter, we talked about the importance of specializing in niche markets. Since consultants are becoming more and more specialized, the websites of some of them now cater to niche markets; others, to as broad a client base as possible. You need to use more innovative and valuable methods and content to attract users to your own site. Set up your web page and take advantage of advertising your consulting services any way you can. You can include your newsletters or articles about your products or services, a list of clients served, and your contact information.

JUDICIOUS USE OF THE INTERNET

Although using the Internet and information technology is a blessing, it can be a curse. If you are not disciplined in how you approach the medium, you lose time, and that equates to lost money and opportunity to do other necessary things.

How often have you gone to the web, pulled up information, and found yourself hours later reading other material with no direct relevance to the reason you first logged on?

Have a purpose when you are searching online. Watch the time. Budget it just like money, because it is.

USEFULNESS OF THE WEB

Networking with others is a great feature of the web. No trip to cyberspace would be complete without interacting with "real" people through bulletin boards or chat rooms dedicated to the topic of changing careers. Communicating with others through the Internet helps you in several ways.

First, you can pick up tips on changing careers, such as becoming an independent consultant. Second, you can communicate with people who are already working in a business you are considering. Third, you can network with people who might be able to help you. For example, to communicate with live people via the Internet about their jobs, including the associated rewards and stresses, visit JobProfiles.com (www.jobprofiles.com). Click a category such as "Consulting" to see a list of related jobs, and then click a job on the list to get a real person's overview of the job's challenges, stresses, and rewards.

Many print magazines are also available online. Most of the online magazines include a few or more sample articles from which you can glean valuable tips and tricks for finding a job. Since our focus is on consulting, here are a number of useful websites you can access to gain information:

- www.EntrepreneurMag.com
  This is the online version of *Entrepreneur Magazine*. It features in-depth perspectives on the financial markets, industries, trends, technology, and people guiding the economy. It includes articles, forums, and chat rooms for the self-employed businessperson.
- www.fastcompany.com
  Fast Company is a business guide that includes information essential to anyone switching careers. It also contains a virtual community of professional organizations. Remember that you want to consider joining a professional organization, and this website may be of help to you for that alone. If you get involved in an appropriate organization, you can get advice, useful tips, and even referrals.
- www.forbes.com
  Forbes is a popular business magazine, also available online. It has practical financial advice and smart tips to manage your money and contains information on business, trends, and global markets.
- www.homebusinessmag.com
  As a beginner consultant starting your home-based business, turn to the online version of *Home Business Magazine*. This site has valuable information on business opportunities, business start-ups, and, in particular, setting up your home office.
- www.successmagazine.com
  Since achieving success is your ultimate goal as an independent consultant, this online version of *Success Magazine* provides articles, support, and success stories for new entrepreneurs. These provide you with motivation and interest to forge ahead with your consulting aspirations.
- www.workingtoday.org
  Since you will be part of America's independent workforce, the magazine *Working Today* is for you. Its website represents the needs and concerns of an independent workforce through advocacy, information, and service.

These are only a few of the best websites that you can access. You will discover more useful sites as you continue to use this technology, which is only one part of the many marketing techniques you may be using. It is probably the most effective, however, because it facilitates your reaching out to a larger audience and efficient because it makes it easy for you and others (potential clients included) to search for specific information.

Other uses of the Internet besides marketing let you:

- find general small business sites, financing sites, and marketing sites;
- qualify for a loan online;
- use the web to host virtual meetings, set up a newsletter, and more;
- manage your money online.

QUALIFY FOR A LOAN ONLINE

Chapter 7 discusses getting funding in a conventional way, like physically going to a bank or other financial institution. You can also obtain financing online. This is probably still new to many people, but an excellent alternative to look into.

A few years ago, the process of obtaining financing was pretty much etched in stone. You would go to the bank, sit nervously at the desk of a loan officer, answer a barrage of questions, and then hope for the best.

Sometimes the approval process took many days, during which you anxiously sifted through your daily mail, searching for a letter from the bank. Then came the advent of applying for loans over the telephone. Local and national lending companies began to offer applicants the convenience of talking with loan officers from the comfort of their homes or offices. This method of loan application quickly became popular and is still widely used today.

With the Internet, ready access to an applicant's computerized financial records and credit reports allows banks to provide quick turnarounds on loan applications; in some cases, lenders can provide answers within a few hours. A quick trip to the bank to sign on the dotted line usually seals the deal.

Today, thanks to the Internet, applying for a loan is easier than ever. A quick keyword search for the word "loan" at a popular search engine/

portal site such as Yahoo! or Google renders a few thousand website matches. Of course, not all of these sites offer online applications for financing, but the number of companies that do offer online loan information and applications is growing steadily. The Internet is regarded as a serious tool for business.

In addition to online applications, many financial services websites offer a variety of tools that can be helpful to users prior to the application process. Some sites offer loan comparison utilities that allow you to determine how your current loan stacks up against other available loan products. Many sites also offer payment calculators that show you how much you should expect to pay per month on a loan based on the amount you borrow, the interest rate, and the terms of the loan. Such tools are easy to use and give you a wealth of free information that was not readily available to the average person before the proliferation of sites on the World Wide Web. For good examples of these financial tools, check out E-LOAN's website (www.eloan.com).

The Internet helps new consultants with:

FINDING BUSINESS OPPORTUNITIES

Several sites are focused on small businesses like your start-up consultancy. Check out what the federal government has to offer. The U.S. Small Business Administration (SBA) at www.sba.gov has some great information. The SBA is dedicated to providing customer-oriented, full-service programs and accurate, timely information to the entrepreneurial community.

STARTING A BUSINESS

Check out, www.startupbiz.com to find resources for people who want to start their own business. This site also offers free advice for naming your business and marketing.

ADVERTISING YOUR BUSINESS

Before you advertise your consulting services, determine your business scope and prospective clientele. Are you going to provide your products or services locally or globally? If you plan to consult locally, you are probably better off advertising using standard regional channels, such as your local newspaper, yellow pages—or if you have the money—radio and TV.

COMPARING INSURANCE RATES

You read earlier about being careful when selecting insurance to best meet your needs. You know that you make the decisions, not the insurance agent. You can also use the Internet to compare insurance rates, but this is a real challenge. Many of the major insurance companies that have websites make it difficult to obtain precise figures because rates vary with location and other factors. They do a nice job of answering questions, presenting insurance packages, and promoting their services, but most of them direct you to the phone or the agent nearest you.

One of the few companies that actually offers online quotes is Prudential (www.prudential.com); however, for legal purposes, it does not offer quotes for Florida and Utah. Once you are at this website, click on the "Insurance Quote" link. Continue to follow the instructions, and at the end of the process you should see a dollar amount. In the future, more insurance companies will realize the convenience of this service and make it widely available—just as travel rates let you search the cheapest fare to any destination.

COMPARING LOAN RATES

You could visit each bank individually on the Internet and search for their current loan rates, or you could visit www.bankrate.com. Most of the institutions listed there have links to their individual websites, and phone numbers are included for your convenience. This website is also loaded with useful "how-to" information, as well as assorted checkers and calculators.

KEY POINTS

- Use the Internet as one of the most effective tools to market yourself, to look for consulting opportunities, and to find financing information.
- Obtain financing online, or look for information about it, to make processing faster and easier.
- Manage your finances electronically to facilitate your tasks, such as setting up an online banking account or finding loan rates online.

Chapter Ten
Interviewing Clients and Establishing Relations

It takes two to speak the truth—one to speak and one to hear.
—**Henry David Thoreau**

A thorough interview of clients and your guidance are crucial for a successful business relationship. This includes the scope and objectives of the work to be performed, the deliverables, and any other tasks. Both parties must fully understand each other's expectations and allocations of resources for the stated work. You will need to answer the following questions:

- What are your deliverables or outputs?

  Does the client expect written materials in a certain electronic format, in hard copy, or both? My friend and business partner, Mary, has expertise in video production and multimedia. If a client hires her to produce a video, she works closely with the client to ensure that her output (a video) meets specifications.

- What is the client's timeline?

  Nowadays, you can use project management software, like Microsoft Project, to establish your timelines for each deliverable. This software is easy to set up and manage, and it is a good tool to also send your client so that he or she can follow where you are on the project. Are you on target? Will you meet deadlines?

- What are the client's priorities?

  In every project, the client establishes priorities. What needs to be done first and when? And in what format?

- What other work or events might derail the current plan of action and milestones?

  You should always plan ahead in case unexpected problems occur. You might miss a deadline, have computer problems, a person working on the project might get sick, or something gets lost in the mail.

- Who is your designated contact person in the company and what is his commitment and availability to review interim submissions of your work, while providing guidance and timely feedback?

  It is essential to have your client's support. Some clients want to be kept abreast of key outputs and easily make themselves or their staff available for review of materials.

Clients may:

- know precisely what they want, but not what it takes to get the tasks done;
- have a vision, but no roadmap or tool kit by which to reach that vision;
- have an idea, but no expertise;
- have expertise, but little if any time or personnel resources to commit to a solution.

PURPOSE OF THE INTERVIEW

When you go for your initial interview with your first potential client, be sure to define yourself. Remember that you are what you sell; you sell a benefit, you are not selling your smile, handshake, or gray suit. What's your product? You're solving a problem and the solution to that problem is your product. You are selling that solution because it is of recognizable benefit to your client's business.

BEFORE THE INTERVIEW

Talk to the prospective client by phone before you set up your meeting. Here are some questions I recommend that you ask on the phone:

- What does the client want to discuss during the meeting?
- Who is the client or decision-maker for this project?
- Who else will be at the meeting and what are their roles?
- How much time will you have?
- Who requested the meeting?

This will be the first sign of where your responsibility lies. How much time the client sets aside for the meeting gives an early indication of the importance of the project to the client. You get a different message if you hear, "We have half an hour," than if you hear, "We have as much time as we need."

Clarify what outcome is expected from the meeting. Is this a meeting to decide how to get started or whether to do anything at all? Will a proposal be required from you? Dealing with these issues before the meeting gives you a better understanding of what the meeting will be about. It also signals to the client that you are a responsible participant in the process and not just an extra pair of hired hands.

DURING THE INTERVIEW

When you meet with the client to begin contracting, the key question is who is the client? Most projects have multiple clients, only one of whom might be the decision-maker. One of the rules of contracting is that you cannot contract with someone who's out of the room.

In general, the client(s) on a project is (are) people who:

- attend the initial planning meeting;
- set the objectives for the project;
- approve any action to be taken;
- receive the interim and/or final report on the results of your work.

This means the client can be a person, a top management team, or a whole department that you work with through a representative planning group. The manager who signs the proposal has ultimate or "signature" authority on decisions and on acceptance of the consultant's outputs. If there's more than one client, try to have at least one meeting with each person who is part of initiating this project. This allows you to get additional information on what each of them wants from you and whether what you are planning will satisfy the group.

117

AT THE END OF THE INTERVIEW
Here are three suggestions to keep in mind.

1. Ask how you and the client will know if you are successful. It may be an unanswerable question, but at least asking it will clarify the client's expectations. At best, it will give you guidance on how to structure the project.
2. Ask for feedback on how the client feels about the project, the meeting, and you. Ask, "How do you feel about the meeting—any reservations?" And, "How do you feel about what I have said and my approach to this—any reservations?" Leave aside 20 minutes to discuss these questions. It may take only two minutes, but if these two questions do uncover new issues, it is best to discuss them now.
3. Close the sale. Closing the sale means getting the prospect to say "yes" and pick up the pen to sign your contract.

Phases of consulting
Identifying a series of phases makes it easier for you to determine whether you are going to get the project or not, and tells you what you need to do in each phase.

Table 14. Phases of Consulting

Consulting phases	Definition
Select	Identify groups qualified to be your clients (e.g., professional associations, industry lists) to be contacted by phone, through sales calls, or direct mail campaigns.
Contact	Talk with prospective clients, those potentially interested in your product or service.
Qualify	Identify the results each prospective client needs.
Introduce	Introduce yourself and your capabilities.
Propose	Prepare and submit a proposal.
Close	Ask client for decision.
Perform	Carry out the assignment.

DEALING WITH CLIENTS
Once you land a contract with your client and you start working on the project, ensure that you put your client first. Communicate well;

provide guidance and innovative solutions; continue to understand your client's needs and ask for feedback; focus on the client's vision (where does he want to go from here); have the client sign off on all stages of the contract.

Develop a system that enables you to follow up with your clients on a regular basis. Keep in touch with them by email, phone, and mail, and encourage them to call you to ask for help, advice, and suggestions—or even just to say hello.

You may not always have ideal clients; some might be difficult, demanding, or just plain impossible to work with on a daily basis. However, there are ways to improve client/consultant relationships and to keep everyone happy. How do you effectively deal with clients who are not easy to work with and will require your patience to pull a project through?

There are some strategies to use when dealing with, communicating with, and negotiating with clients. How do you deal with a demanding one, for instance?

What you really want to know here is, does this demanding client have a good handle on his own requirements? He has come to you, but if he doesn't really know what he wants, then he'll continue to be demanding and may never be satisfied. You may not even ever see financial gain from helping him.

First, spend some time with him to get clarity. Perhaps he needs to go back to the drawing board and figure out what he actually needs. Either way, it's important that you try to help him without spending too much of your time just getting him to that point of realization that he should have been at before he hired you. Otherwise, remaining profitable will be difficult for you.

Second, will you do more business with the client in the future? If so, then that makes him even more worth your time and effort to build a successful relationship with. You do not really want to lose any potential client, but it's especially important to hang on to those that will likely keep coming back to you. And no one knows your business better than you–you'll likely be able to quickly analyze the situation and figure out whether or not this client will need you for future business as well.

KEY POINTS

- Address the issues identified if the scope of work expands or needs to be modified to meet challenges and opportunities.
- Be part of the client's solution, not part of the problem.
- Stay alert, stay in touch, and get the attention of the client as soon as possible should you need to readdress the tasks assigned or the timing of the delivery.
- Ask for guidance on other matters that can affect the project.
- Get advice on who should write the contract, points that must be included, whether it's enough to have a client sign an acceptance of your proposal, penalties to write in, and recommend times for these contract procedures to take place.
- Follow up, before you accept other contracts, with the prospective client by phone as negotiations continue.
- Solve the problems and put forth a quality solution or product deliverable. Make your client your priority.

Chapter Eleven
Setting and Collecting Fees and Billing Options

Don't judge each day by the harvest you reap but by the seeds that you plant.
—**Robert Louis Stevenson**

Setting fees is one of the most important steps in building and maintaining your consulting business. Since you are selling your services for the first time, you want to be viewed as responsible, reliable, knowledgeable, desirable, and honest. Your fee is an effective measure that conveys the real value of your services. Fee setting is also an important element in marketing your services. Set a reasonable fee that you believe is commensurate with your abilities.

SETTING YOUR FEES
There are several ways to set your fees:

HOURLY RATE
Find out how many other consultants in your geographic area charge for the same type of work you do.

Build your rate from the bottom up; if you have been working as an employee for a number of years, maintain your previous pay rate, add your expenses for health and insurance coverage and other benefits, then add $10 to cover other expenses.

Or build your rate from top down; if you want to gross $70,000 a year from your consulting efforts, and you estimate working 1,200 hours, you divide $70,000 by 1,200. In this case, you have to charge at least $58–$60 to reach your goal. Or, apply the rule of third: you should take your hourly wage as a full-time employee and multiply it by three to arrive at the fee that you want to charge as a consultant. Example, if you earn $35 an hour as an instructional designer, as a consultant you should charge your client $105 an hour. As a consultant you pay yourself a wage (1/3 of the total rate), pay for health and life insurance coverage, retirement plans, and so on (another 1/3 of the total rate), plus set aside some amount for profit (the last 1/3 of the total rate).

Remember to convince your client that you are worth what you are charging. Setting your fees too low sends the message that you don't value your services adequately. It also sends a message to your potential client that you may not be able to provide quality service or you're not the best person for the job.

Suzanne sometimes raises her own rate based on what she considers to be "extenuating circumstances" (short notice, scope creep, handholding of client, etc.). She usually starts with a rate supplied by the client. Ideally, Suzanne prefers to charge on an estimated project cost basis to give her greater leeway when dealing with project surprises and overruns.

PER-ITEM OR PER-PROJECT BASIS

Pricing on a per-item or per-project basis allows you to focus your work on results that you will achieve for the client and the value that your client will receive from your services. A couple of years ago I spent fifteen days and three hours to design and develop a pre-sales workshop, which entailed creating facilitator and user guides, handouts, activity materials, and attend pilot training. The rate agreed on was $640 a day on the per-project basis.

RETAINER BASIS

A retainer is a fixed amount of money that a client agrees to pay, in advance, to secure the services of a consultant. This fee is not associated with the success of a project or based on achieving a particular result. A retainer is often paid one time, in a lump sum, or on an ongoing basis, typically monthly or quarterly.

When you are just starting your career as a consultant, it is wise to start on smaller jobs or tasks with the client to establish trust and credibility. Once established, you ultimately want to move toward a retainer fee where you will get a guaranteed amount of money regardless of the amount of work you provide for the client. To be kept on retainer, you need to take on higher-level work with the client, introduce a new project idea when the opportunity arises, and ensure monthly follow-ups with the client to find out how your work had been received and if the client needs additional help.

Once you have established trust and credibility and get a retainer agreement, make sure that the terms are specific: roles and responsibilities are defined, work that you will do specifically, and the maximum number of hours you will work under this agreement. What is vital is that you provide the best value for your services and not shortchange yourself. At the end of this retainer agreement, you and the client can evaluate your work and time spent working to determine if adjustments to the next retainer agreement should be made. Being on a retainer protects from the scenario of "feast and famine" that consultants, especially new ones, usually experience.

Setting your fees right from the beginning will help you get started on the right foot because starting too low will:

- cost you more in the long run because you are forced to work at a rate of pay that may not be enough to support your consulting business;
- set you up for future business at the same low, unrealistic rates;
- imply that you offer poor service.

Charging a low fee can mean that you are overanxious to get your first consulting project. The reality is that you may not be able to sustain your expenses, and this could in fact affect the quality of your service.

There are many ways to set fees. The three most common arrangements (approximately 85 percent of them) are daily rate, fixed price, and fixed price plus expenses. Arriving at the right fee for your business involves several steps:

1. Establish your daily labor rate. This is the value of your time and the time of others if you have subcontractors. It is important to create a price schedule for each type of consulting service you

offer. This way, you know how much to charge for yourself and how much to pay subcontractors, if you need other professionals to help out with such projects.

2. Determine your overhead, which is the expense of being in business. If you work from home, you may be able to charge your client a little less because you won't have the same overhead as if you were renting an office.

3. Determine what percentage of your budget should go toward marketing, because marketing expenses are part of the cost of being in business.

4. Set your profit, which is the value of the risks you take, by being in business. Remember that being a consultant is "feast or famine," so you want to make sure that you cover yourself for the full year.

In today's market, few consultants accept daily fees of less than $600, although that varies somewhat with local conditions and individual policies. For example, $600 works out to $75 per hour for an eight-hour working day, but not every $600-per-day consultant charges for overtime. Some may charge $75 per hour but charge extra for overtime, weekends, and holidays.

Let's take a hypothetical case. You decide you ought to pay yourself $25 an hour (or $52,000 annual salary), but you estimate that your first year's overhead rate will be about 125 percent. That means you must charge $56 an hour ($450 cost per day + $50 pre-tax profit = $500 a day). This rate is well below the competitive rate in today's market. In fact, it is extremely low compared to what consultants can obtain in bigger cities like Boston, Washington, D.C., New York, and San Francisco. To help set your fee, consider these questions:

1. How long will the project take?

2. Can you do it yourself or will you need additional help? If you do it yourself, how many hours will it take you to complete the project? Double it. (This is the rule of thumb I've heard over and over.)

3. If you need additional help, how many people do you need and are you prepared for the time of managing them and reviewing their work?

4. How much will you have to pay each person who helps you on the project?
5. Will there be expenses? If so, should the client approve all of these expenses, or just those over a certain amount?
6. How many extra hours should you allow for the unexpected?
7. How will your project fit into your overhead calculations and profit-making goals?

BILLING RATES

The daily billing rate has three components: labor, overhead, and profit. Within the overhead component are fixed, variable, and direct expenses.

DAILY LABOR

The daily labor rate starts with deciding your annual worth. You then convert the annual amount to a daily amount, to which is added overhead and profit. This determines your fee.

For example, take your projected or present annual income, say, $70,000. Decide if you want to work the full 261 working days a year. Then calculate your daily labor rate by dividing $70,000 by 261. Your daily labor rate is $270 (rounded to the nearest dollar from $268).

OVERHEAD

Overhead includes the expenses that you have regardless of how much work you do. Overhead expenses increase as your business expands. What is typically included in overhead? Rent, equipment you purchase or lease, and marketing. If you are working solo, additional overhead expenses include whatever services you subcontract, such as billing, typing, and other administrative services. Nowadays, however, you can do most of these administrative chores yourself with the availability of technology, which makes operating on your own, or with only some help, easier and quicker than it used to be.

FIXED AND VARIABLE EXPENSES

Fixed expenses are those expenses for overhead used by you regardless of the volume of your workload. Variable expenses are those that can change in relation to the volume of your workload; subcontracting fees are one example.

Subcontractors do the work that consultants do not have the time, expertise, or inclination to do. By using subcontractors, you can make money on the difference between what you pay a subcontractor and what you are paid by your client. Many subcontractors struggle with the fact that their time is getting billed at a rate higher than the amount they receive, but the subcontractor is in effect paying you for finding the work. As a consultant, you become more like an employer in this case. You become responsible for the subcontractor. In other words, you get paid extra for finding the work and taking responsibility for the whole project. If you work with subcontractors, make sure that you add a non-compete clause in their contracts. A non-compete clause discourages subcontractors from working directly with your client within a certain period of time, anywhere from six months to two years, after their role with your client ends. In the event that the subcontractor does engage in work with your client, the clauses often stipulate that you can collect a "sales representation fee" for the time and money you invested in having developed that client—usually a percent of all fees the subcontractor bills to your client. You'll want an attorney to draft or at least review any contracts your business depends on for maintaining its financial health.

Some of my independent consultant-friends hire subcontractors when they are under time constraints and do not have the precise expertise to perform each part of the job. The subcontractors' work is transparent to the client. What is important is that the client gets the final product as specified. The client is not involved with subcontractor fees and individual outputs.

DIRECT EXPENSES

Direct expenses depend on the type of work you do. These are costs arising directly from your work on a particular project. They might include the daily labor rates of any subcontractors, travel expenses related to your project, long-distance phone calls, and supplies for reports and presentations.

PROFIT

Over and above your daily labor rate and overhead, you should charge to make a profit. However, a profit might not materialize during your first year of consulting because of upfront marketing and other start-up costs. Even if you invest little in your business when you are starting, you are nevertheless investing your time, which ultimately translates to money.

Profit is the reason you are in business. It is your reward for taking business risks and assuming the responsibilities and pressures of ownership. Profit for consultants generally ranges from 10 percent to 30 percent of your actual income.

See *Figure 1* for a sample calculation of a 15 percent profit, if that is what you want to add to your daily labor rate and overhead.

Daily labor rate	$270
Overhead	$400
Subtotal	$670

Figure 1: Daily labor rate and overhead

In *Figure 2*, you determine your profit by multiplying the subtotal of $670 by 15 percent. Your daily profit is $100.

$670 x .15 = $100 (rounded)

Figure 2: Daily profit

Some clients, especially government agencies, have policies that do not allow you to receive profits.

Let's look at the computed daily labor rate from *Figure 1* above and see how the numbers change by adding the 15 percent profit.

Daily labor rate	$270
Overhead	$400
Profit	$130
Subtotal	$800

Figure 3: Computed daily labor rate

Ensure that the profit you plan to charge is acceptable to your client's policies during the fee-setting phase. Some consultants use another means to get the additional profit without showing it as a profit. They create an additional category called General and Administrative Expenses (G&A). Larger companies use G&A expenses to account for overhead-type costs like corporate-wide auditing and communication.

Billing rates are not limited to daily rate, overhead, and profit. Based on my experience working with consultants, other payment structures are in use, such as: fixed price contract, fixed fee plus expenses, and time and materials. There are also retainer fees and cost reimbursements.

Here are brief descriptions of these other billing approaches:

- Fixed-price contract
  This is very simple. After you determine your client's needs, you say that you are willing to charge a flat dollar fee: the fixed price you set to be accepted by your client before the contract is drawn. The upside to a fixed price contract is that if you work efficiently and provide services that cost less than you estimated, you get more profit. The downside is that if your expenses are higher than estimated, you lose some profit. Your client doesn't stand to lose in a fixed-price contract. The risk is all yours.

- Fixed price plus expenses
  When the direct expenses are difficult or impossible to estimate, you can submit the direct labor charge as a fixed fee, but your client is liable for the direct expenses.

In my last contract hiring another consultant where I was the client, we used the fixed price plus expenses arrangement. The total project costs came to $33,700, with the project costs at $32,000 and $1,700 for travel, mailing, and printing expenses. As agreed by both parties, we made three equal quarterly payments. The first payment started in June, the second in August, and the third and last payment in October. The project went smoothly from proposal to contract and to completion.

Fixed Price Plus Expenses

May	June	July	Aug	Sept	Oct	Total Contract
Proposal approved	$10,666 contract signed	—	$10,666	—	$10,666 + $1,700 expenses	$33,700

Figure 4: Fixed Price plus Expenses

- Time and Material (T&M)
  This contract works exactly like the daily labor rate contract with a couple of exceptions. You absorb the cost and expenses of the active project, and bill your client in installments. The payment structure can be monthly or fixed installments that coincide

with specific outputs, depending on the length and complexity of the project. If the client agrees to pay in three installments, he makes the first payment when the contract is signed, the second payment when the first output is delivered, and the third payment when all the outputs are completed and delivered.

- Retainers
  This is a contract wherein the consultant agrees to make his or her services available to the client as the need arises. A retainer arrangement works only if you are good at estimating. If you underestimate the client's needs, the result is poor cash inflow. Larger companies use this type of contract, whereas smaller companies may need specialized consulting regularly.

Calculation of Profit and General and Administrative Expenses (G&A)

Using the same numbers from *Figure 1*, the next figure presents an amended computation of daily rate. Calculate the 15 percent profit based on the subtotal. You want 5 percent to go to profit and 10 percent to G&A, which is also used for salaries of clerical and administrative personnel, supplies, and other expenses.

Daily labor rate	$270
Overhead	$400
Subtotal	$670

Figure 5: Calculation of profit and G&A expenses

If you calculated correctly, here's how the amended computation of your daily rate would look:

Daily labor rate	$270
Overhead	$400
Subtotal	$670
Profit	$ 35
G&A	$ 67
Daily fee	$772

Figure 6: Amended computation of daily rate

This is really the simplest way to calculate your daily fee if you are a beginning consultant.

COLLECTIONS

Collecting fees is essential for you because you are running a business. In your first year of consulting, you may have limited cash available to tide you over while you await payment.

Especially with lengthy processing times for paperwork, not being paid on a timely basis is common. Other factors that contribute to difficulties in collecting fees include a payment schedule tied to submitting your reports, and reports being tied to the timetable that both you and the client set up at the beginning of the project.

For small billings, you might not have problems collecting, but when larger fees are involved, litigation could be necessary. That's why a detailed contract for larger fees is invaluable and is a safety net for you. On the other hand, if your contract has a written arbitration clause, it might help you get your money without resorting to legal means. Going to court is more costly than arbitration; you don't want this when you are just starting. You could be bankrupt before you reach any of your goals.

Be sure your contract, as well as your invoices, include a statement of your terms. Remember that your fees are your income and your proof that you can make it as a consultant. More often than not, potential consultants do not understand fees very well. The media reports that consultants charge anywhere between $100 an hour to $2,000 a day. Potential consultants assume that these rates are pure profit. They are not. With some quick calculations, using 2000 work hours a year x $100 an hour, you can project an annual gross income of $200,000 a year.

Collecting your fees in a timely manner gives you more cash assets. Here are three salient tips for working with a client to ensure you are paid on time:

1. Discuss payment when the consulting agreement is signed.
   Even if your payment terms are clearly spelled out in your written consulting agreement, reiterate these terms orally upon signing the agreement. If the transaction takes place by mail, mention the payment terms in your letter of transmittal. This lets the client

know your expectations up front, and provides the opportunity to respond with payment options.

2. Invoice immediately.

You should invoice immediately upon completion of every deliverable. This usually facilitates faster approval and processing than if you send the invoice later by mail. In some cases, however, companies tell you to submit your invoice at the end of the month in which you've rendered your service or completed your project; you will usually receive payment within forty-five days.

3. Consistent follow-up.

If your payment terms are net ten days after invoice, follow-up after ten days, plus a reasonable mail delivery time, to find out the status of your payment. Many times the check is in process and is going through the client's normal accounting cycle. Keeping abreast of late invoices will prevent a backlog of cash flow.

Without successful fee collection, you cannot pay your own bills. You then run the risk of creditors foreclosing on you. Oddly, new or potential consultants often ignore fee collections until it is too late. Three common situations can put you out of business before you even begin to achieve success:

1. When you first open your practice, you "carry" too many clients—assuming you already have a loyal following. You fulfill all your contracts but allow clients to defer payments. As a result, you have little cash inflow to meet your business and personal obligations.

2. You do not watch your collection rate, which is crucial to profitability. By not monitoring your collection rate, you have no way of finding out when it falls to dangerous levels.

3. You do not follow-up on unpaid bills. You are reluctant to ask for money, even though avoiding the topic creates a desire for the client and you to avoid each other. Avoidance leads to non-payment and potentially dissolves your relationship. Forget repeat business!

Because your business depends on successful fee collection, you should devote considerable attention to it.

BILLING OPTIONS

The three most common billing options are self-explanatory:

1. On delivery of work, invoice for work accomplished to date.
2. Arrange for a flat weekly or monthly advance payment.
3. Contract for payment upon completion of the project.

As an independent consultant, Suzanne has to be responsible for everything related to estimating costs, communicating about overages, tracking time/dollars, billing, and collecting—no one else will do this for you. Some clients are poor at follow-up once the contract is signed; not intentionally, it's just not their focus. That means the consultant has to be the timekeeper, the bookkeeper, the accounts receivable clerk, and the collection agency, if necessary. This is very different from getting a regular paycheck every other week, with the correct amount of FICA and insurance taken out.

KEY POINTS

- Set your fee by taking appropriate steps, starting with setting a value on your expertise and experience to establish your daily labor rate. Then identify your overhead, determine the percentage of your budget that should go into marketing, and, of course, calculate your profit.
- Prepare a fixed price schedule to include direct labor and direct expenses to determine your total fixed price every month.
- Discuss payment with each client when you sign the consulting agreement. Payment terms may vary. Clients offer billing options based on their practice.

Chapter Twelve
Writing Proposals

Every act rewards itself.
—**Ralph Waldo Emerson**

One of the key consulting skills is writing, whether for proposals, contracts, reports, or presentations. Since a proposal is your marketing or sales tool—which you cannot bill for—you want to ensure that you follow a format or structure that explains in-depth the job you will perform. Anyone can learn how to write a proposal; what's important are the facts. Present your proposal orally and in writing, both of which may be required in most cases. After you sign the contractual agreement and you start working for the client, you will be asked to write progress and final reports. These are part of the job and are therefore billable.

INITIAL CONSULTATIONS
New consultants tend to give away free consulting in their attempts to win a project or to please a client. Consultants also give away free consulting during diagnostic work. They hope that by providing free consultation to demonstrate their expertise, the client will hire them. More often than not, a client hires others to resolve the problem or implement the project you identified free of charge.

Is sharing unpaid expertise a smart move? Sometimes yes; most times, no. Why? Frequently, the client will phone you after your initial client interview to seek your advice about the project or about a new problem, saying that a visit is not necessary. To avoid providing free advice indefinitely, after a period of time, it is expedient to suggest that the client put you on a retainer so that you can continue to advise him.

You have two options when faced with this situation, either bill the client for your time spent on the phone, or secure a retainer from which you bill as the client chooses to use your services. DO NOT provide this service for free. Avoid problems by NOT giving away free consulting, or, in simple consulting street talk, "giving away the store."

PROPOSAL DEFINED

A proposal is a selling document. It is intended to be informative and appealing to convince clients to hire you. Proposals are very important because they let your potential clients know that you understand their problems as well as they do. Proposals state what you plan to do for the clients and state in *specific* terms the anticipated results and potential benefits.

PROPOSAL FORMAT

You will find that structural format and tools enhance the readability of your proposal. Make it short and to the point. Few people can read a thirty-to-forty-page document without getting sleepy. Make your readers' job easier so they will be more interested in reading your complete proposal. Paragraphing breaks up the body copy and helps the eye flow down the page. Headlines spaced within the body "chunk" the text and make the content more meaningful and memorable. Leave lots of white space.

GETTING ORGANIZED

Before you write a proposal, you have to organize what you want to write about. Based on Shipley Associates' *Proposal Guide**, a sound, well-conceived organization makes the actual writing easier, especially for consultants with limited confidence in their writing skills. To make the writing easier, start by creating an outline that covers each section or topic within your proposal and use templates in your software program to help organize your messages before you draft the actual text.

---

* *Proposal Guide for Business Development and Sales Professionals.* 2001-2003 Shipley Associates, Business Development Services, Farmington, UT.

WRITING A GOOD PROPOSAL

1. **Keep the structure clear and logical.** Sometimes, especially for large industry, government, and competitive contracts where bidding is allowed, the client will tell you the structure of the proposal. Follow the structure that your client requires.

2. **Use a professional but friendly style of writing.** If you are writing a proposal letter, you can be somewhat informal, as long as you avoid stepping over professional bounds. An effective writing style can enhance your chances of being hired.

3. **Don't spring surprises in your proposal.** Restraint is a challenge because after your initial client interview, you frequently get new insight and ideas different from what you and your client originally planned and agreed upon. Even if these new ideas are good, do not add them to your proposal unless you receive the "go ahead" from the client. Why? He or she may want to sell it to senior management first. Clear new ideas before you put too much effort into the contract. You can always go back to the client and propose modifications or additions after you get the contract.

4. **Double-check the main points of your proposal with the client before you send it.** If it's a short letter proposal, you can call the client and read it to him or her over the phone. However, this may not work in all situations. For instance, this approach may not be allowed for government and industrial contracts that require competitive bidding, but there's no harm in asking first. It is always in your best interest that your proposal is on the right track; you cannot assume that you will be allowed to make changes after the client has received it.

WRITING A WINNING PROPOSAL

Proposal writing has nothing to do with creative writing, nor does it have anything to do with stringing together descriptive adjectives and superlatives. Proposal writing can be learned; it does not require the skills of an English professor or a polished writer. You need to gather facts. If you are writing for a public sector assignment, you need excellent intuition and insight in addition to your fact-gathering ability. The type of marketing or promotion you use varies by group.

Keep four things in mind when writing a proposal:

1. **No generalizations.** A proposal loaded with generalities is a sure loser. Stick to specifics; proposals get down to details.
2. **No hyperbole.** Saying, "My firm is the greatest" without proper back-up is not a way to win a business.
3. **Minimal adjectives.** You should avoid using too many adjectives. Straightforward nouns and verbs are more effective than weak words that take power from modifiers. Avoid describing procedures in a proposal in glowing terms. Your potential clients are interested only in how you see their problem, how you are going to solve it, and how much it is going to cost.
4. **Keep it simple.** There is a tendency for consultants to try and knock prospects off their feet with buzzwords, jargon, inside terminology, and acronyms; avoid these at all costs. Clients will become perturbed by reading something they do not understand.

PRESENTING YOUR PROPOSAL

Oral presentations should not be a repeat of the written proposal. Instead, pluck out the elements that set you apart from your competitors. Oral presentations are usually limited to thirty minutes or less. Despite the relative shortness of time, use visual aids. Slides (35 mm or overhead from your laptop) can enhance your talk, and if you are not a dynamic speaker, they help make up for your deficiency. Use colors and presentation designs so the slides aren't too confusing.

When you make your presentation, the audience is going to get two distinct impressions that will weigh heavily in their decision-making: (1) your appearance, and (2) your ability to speak. You have to be concerned not only with what you say but also how you say it. A talk littered with non-words, such as "umms" and "ahs" is distracting and seldom gets the message across. Keep your sentences uncomplicated so they'll seem smooth and clear and make you appear competent and articulate.

Your clients may be slow in responding to your proposal. Do not pressure them. Take certain steps to clarify the situation and obtain the desired contract. While you are waiting for a decision, you are losing the opportunity to earn income. This loss is called an opportunity cost, which refers to the costs associated with giving up the opportunity to conduct business with others. You need to add in this cost as part of your overhead or cost of doing business.

For example, if you state in your cover letter that you will contact the clients on the tenth day to answer any questions, you may either be asked further questions or get a "yes" or "no" to your proposal. If the reason for a delayed decision appears unavoidable, you may wish to wait five more business days and then drop in to see the client in person to ask if a decision has been made. This approach may or may not be appropriate in certain situations. Depending on the situation, you might adopt the attitude that you would like to know one way or the other within a certain time. To clients, this may mean you are in demand and might commit to another project if they don't accept your services within the given time.

I once wrote a proposal with the objective of landing a contract to design and develop a Business Process Management Workshop. Initially, the prospective client gave me her requirements and specifications by telephone. I wrote everything down and sent her an email asking her to verify my information. In addition to the proposal, she wanted me to attach a copy of my résumé. She wanted to make sure that whoever worked on the project had an advanced degree and extensive experience in designing and developing training.

After I submitted the proposal, I wasn't sure whether it would be approved. It took about two weeks before the client got back to me. I didn't call her within those two weeks, thinking to give her time to look over the proposal and get the appropriate approvals, since she wasn't the only decision-maker. When the call came, I learned that senior management had given approval and that she was working on a contract to send to me immediately. I got the contract and quickly assembled a team to work with me on the project.

What I'm getting at is that every proposal is different. It is not and should not be a boilerplate, a one size fits all. You have to tailor it to your client's specific needs. What I felt important to include in the above proposal were four things: (1) the service to be performed, (2) the fee to be charged for the service, (3) the time payment was due, and (4) the milestones—when each output or deliverable was due to the client. Along the way, I talked to my client weekly to update her on the status of the project.

PROPOSAL SAMPLES

The length, depth, and breadth of your proposal greatly depend on the nature of your business and your client's expectations. For example, if you are a computer consultant and your client hired you to install a new hard drive on his computer, you do not need a forty-page proposal detailing all the benefits of the new hard drive. Your client may just ask you to discuss your experience, how much you charge for your services, and when you can do the job that the client hired you to do. However, for complex multi-year proposals, you have to prioritize specific details that could result in a forty-page proposal.

A proposal will either be a short letter-type proposal that is one to two pages long, or a longer, narrative-type proposal, ten or more pages in length.

LETTER-TYPE PROPOSAL

A letter-type proposal presents the most important information that your potential client needs to know. You can submit this to your client via email, fax, or an actual printed and signed letter.

A letter-type proposal is particularly useful for projects that are simple, are short in duration, or don't cost your client very much money, and should include the following:

1. **The point**
   Get directly to what you are offering by focusing on results and on the client's advantage of working with you.

2. **Proposed project**
   Provide a brief description of your project.

3. **Anticipated outcomes**
   Summarize your expected outcomes.

4. **Action plan**
   Outline the steps you will take to reach your anticipated outcomes.

5. **Price**
   Provide your client with the bottom line, which may include your fees and reimbursable expenses.

6. **Payment terms**

   Break down your pay system instead of providing a lump sum payment.

7. **Next steps**

   Explain what the client needs to do to initiate the project and get you started. As soon as the client signs on the dotted line, you have a binding contract.

Table 15
Sample Letter-Type Proposal

Mr. John Smith
DEG Sales Company
3233 Lake Shore Drive
Virginia Beach, VA 23456

Dear Mr. Smith:

ABC Consulting Company is delighted to have the opportunity to respond to your requirement for a solution that will dramatically increase your sales volume over a short period of time.

The accompanying proposal provides an extremely comprehensive response to all of the requirements outlined by DEG Sales Company over our discussion in the last several weeks.

DEG Sales Company Challenge

Your sales team has forty-five sales professionals—all hired with a specific combination of education, skills, and experience that they share in common, and which should assure that all are highly qualified and successful in their positions. However, sales performance across the team varies widely—from the highest performers who deliver a performance against quota of as much as 140% (the top ten range from 110% to 140%, with an average performance of 125%, to the lower performers, who deliver as little as 80% against quota.

DEG Sales Company has the potential to increase their sales output by a factor of several hundred percent–if they can determine what it is that makes their top performers so much more productive than their

139

average and bottom performers, and if they can use that information to raise the performance of every member of their sales team to the level of their top performers.

Profiles Solution

As discussed, ABC Consulting Company will establish a customized Online Assessment Center (Profiles on the Web) to enable DEG Sales Company to comprehensively assess their sales team. Using the ProfileXT, we will assess your entire team and use our unique success pattern technology to identify the particular combination of attributes that make your top performing sales people so successful. By analyzing the top performers, we will identify the particular combination of learning abilities, behavioral/personality characteristics, and work interests/ motivations that make these people capable of performance as such a higher level than their peers.

As you saw, the proposed Profiles on the Web (POTW) system provides a wide range of "plain English" reports that will allow you and your managers to manage every people decision you ever have to make—but will most particularly help you to:

- Identify candidates with the same unique combination of success characteristics as your current top performers.
- Provide detailed information to sales management on precisely what combination of coaching, training, and management is required to raise the game of each of your average or below average performers to the performance level of your top people.
- Use the success pattern and candidate information you build on your POTW system to more effectively manage succession and career planning activities.

Benefits of the Proposed Solution

1. Exceptional Return on Investment.
2. Extremely low entry costs.
3. Pay-as-you-use model.
4. Proven track record with similar organizations.
5. Fast implementation—no specific training or certificate required.

6. Countrywide support.

7. Inexpensive to take nationwide or globally.

All at ABC Consulting Company are completely committed to dramatically increasing the sales results in DEG Sales Company by several hundred percent in a matter of a few months.

Assuming DEG Sales Company makes a decision to proceed with implementation by May 15th, the solution can be fully implemented by July 1st, with the first concrete results ready to report well in advance of the DEG Sales Company conference planned for Q4.

Many thanks for the opportunity to work with you on what we are certain will be a successful partnership.

Sincerely,
Joseph Doe

Table 16
Sample Elements of a Narrative Proposal

A narrative proposal can run from ten to hundreds of pages. You generally address the same kinds of information as in a letter proposal but in much greater detail.

Below is a summary of a typical narrative proposal:

Part	Definition
Cover Letter	Contains title of the proposal with your contact information (name, phone number, fax number, email address, street address, web site address, etc.).
Title Page	Contains the title of your proposal along with the following information (date, name of your business (if any), your name, your client's name or client's organization).

Continues.

Part	Definition
Table of Contents	Contains topics with page numbers so clients can find their way around your proposal.
Executive Summary	Contains summary of entire proposal in a quick, thirty-second reading; typically a half to one page in length.
Anticipated Outcomes	As in the letter proposal, but with more detail.
Detailed Scope of Work	Presents every task and subtask that you will do.
Project Schedule	Assigns each task presented in the Scope of Work, a start date, duration, and end date. You may present this schedule using a Microsoft Project chart that shows information clearly.
Fee	Provides the work you plan to do and cost. You can present your fee as a monthly flat rate or an hourly fee, and you can make changes if the client wants you to price your work differently.
Qualifications and Experience	Provide a summary of your experience including training, certification, and licenses. In most cases, if several people will do the work, you can attach their résumés.
Résumés	Include key project personnel and make sure to customize each résumé to the requirements of the proposal.
Letters of Reference	Include if client asks for them.

You can also get sample proposal letters from various sources, such as FedBizOpps (government request for proposals), Google, other consultants, business forms from Microsoft, or old copies of proposals from previous jobs. Most customers have a standard legal contract that they will share with you with their terms and conditions. You can follow the same format or customize to request for proposal requirements.

You should also take advantage of the Small Business Associations in your town or city; check your local directory for the address nearest you. SBAs usually provide to small business owners at least two free consulting services. They provide free clinics and seminars to people who are considering starting their own business and also provide you with valuable information on required certifications, taxes, and tapping into state, local, and federal opportunities.

KEY POINTS

- Learn how to write proposals.
- Gather the facts that are critical to writing a winning proposal.
- Listen to your client and determine exact needs. Ask questions for clarification on any issues.
- Include your client's requirements in your proposal. For instance, if your client wants you to include colored photos of hardware and software you will be installing, don't ignore their request.
- Start working on your proposal right away and do not put it off until the last minute.
- Review your proposal before you submit it to your client to ensure it is not sloppily written and that it includes all information.
- Create a database of proposals you've previously submitted because you will be able to recycle information in future proposals and use half of the content as a boilerplate. For example, résumés of your key project personnel may only need minor updates.

Chapter Thirteen
Writing Contracts

The universe never did make sense; I suspect it was built on government contracts.
— **Herman Heinlin, American science fiction writer.**

Contracts are written to confirm consulting agreements between you and the client. They state specifically what the project is, what you are hired to do, and what you will deliver upon project completion. Contracts also serve to protect both parties, ensuring that what is agreed upon is followed.

CONTRACT DEFINED

A contract is the basis by which your obligations, rights, remedies, and payments are clarified. Simply, a contract states what you are bound to do and what you are entitled to receive. Contracts can be oral, written, or implied. Most consultants prefer a written contract for their own protection. A written contract is binding once both parties—client and consultant—sign on the dotted line.

WHAT MAKES A VALID CONTRACT?

- **Offer.** If you submit a proposal or a contract to a client, it constitutes your offer to have the client accept what you propose.
- **Acceptance.** This is your potential client's confirming in writing, his or her acceptance of your proposal letter and contract.

- **Consideration.** This is something of value being promised to you in exchange for your services. It almost always refers to money.
- **Competency.** An agreement will not be considered binding if signed by persons lacking competence to understand the "nature and quality of their actions," such as one party being drunk at the time of accepting and signing the agreement.
- **Legality.** A contract to perform an illegal act is void. For example, if a number of businesses signed an agreement to fix prices for their services and one signatory failed to follow the agreement, the others would not be able to sue for breach of contract as the action agreed to was illegal.

Your consulting agreement should cover the following elements: date, parties by and between, services agreed to, standard for services and products, compensation, ethical standards, evaluation of vendor bids (if applicable), employees of consultant (if applicable), confidential relationship, insurance, indemnification, term and termination, compliance with Safety and Security Regulations, compliance with laws, notices (addresses), proprietary rights, general provisions, and signatures (client and consultant).

WHY YOU NEED A WRITTEN CONTRACT

Here are some of the reasons to choose a written contract, instead of, or in addition to, a simple handshake.

- **Project a professional image.** A written contract enhances your image as a responsible professional and businessperson.
- **Avoid misunderstandings.** It is difficult to remember complex details without having them in writing.
- **Outline terms for payment.** With specific, written terms of payment—such as partial payment each month or at specific stages during the project—clients are likely to wait until the end of the job to pay.
- **Confirm fee for services.** You want to make clear that you are going to be paid for your time and efforts.
- **Communicate.** Good communication is essential for client satisfaction and goodwill.

In summary, you have choices about which type of contract to use, but for the above reasons, and for your own protection, it is wise to ask for a written contract. See Table 17-Sample Letter of Agreement and Table 18-Elements in a Contract.

Table 17
Sample Letter of Agreement
(Use your Letterhead)

Date
Client name and address

Dear _____:
Re: Consulting Agreement
This letter will confirm our mutual understanding of the conditions under which I shall perform certain functions for your company, as follows:

a) Conditions. This agreement will be for a period of ____, starting ____. Either of us may terminate this agreement with thirty (30) days' written notice to the other party. In the event of termination, I shall be compensated for services rendered through the date of termination.

b) Duties. My key duties shall include:
- Review of, analysis of, and recommendations for improvement of the Information systems structure of your Research Division, as detailed in my proposal dated _____.
- Preparation of weekly reports on the progress of the project.
- Preparation of a final report and oral presentation to the management of your company, with recommendations for implementing improvements to your information systems and structure, and the related costs.

c) Compensation. The compensation for my services shall be at the rate of $____ per day, payable as billed. Other out-of-pocket costs, such as travel expenses and secretarial services, shall be billed separately.

147

Enclosed is a copy of this agreement for your records. Please sign the original and return it to this office in the enclosed envelope. If you have any questions, do not hesitate to contact me.

Sincerely,
Leticia Gallares-Japzon
Consultant

Accepted and agreed to:
Juan Valdez

Table 18
Elements of a Contract

Element	Description	Example
Boundaries of your work	Begin with a statement of the problem the client hired you to solve.	I will assess the effectiveness of your Sales Organization structure and see how it can more effectively interface with the Marketing Organization.
Objective of the project	State what it is you are supposed to achieve so you both agree that your consultation is successful. You have to look at solving the client's problem, and/or teaching the client how to solve the problem so he or she and his or her employees can do it themselves the next time the same problem arises.	My objective for this project is to increase the productivity of your sales representatives by 100 percent.
Information and resources you need from client	Be clear about the kind of information you will want access to; e.g., data, roles and responsibilities of employees, resources, workflow, contact person, and so on. If the contact person changes, ask that you be informed of his or her replacement. Also add that the contract price may have to be adjusted for any extra time involved in carrying out your project due to personnel or other changes the client might make.	I will have access to personnel and information, and be apprised of your key wants.

Your role in the project	State how you want to work with your client. If you want close collaboration, this is the place to say so. Your role doesn't have to be explicitly stated; just your intent and spirit.	I shall be equal partners with the client, with a 50/50 share of responsibilities in identifying and analyzing problems, generating solutions, developing action plans, and providing recommendations.
The product you deliver	Specify what you will offer. Will your feedback be oral or in writing? How long will it take to complete the project? How much detail do you understand that the client wants? Will you give the client a list of recommendations?	The outcome of this project will be a ten-page written report that summarizes my key findings and specific recommendations.
The support and involvement you need from the client	Specify what you want from your client to make the project successful. This is where you include the "wants" that you discussed during a face-to-face meeting to ensure issues are resolved.	My client and I agree to present the report to senior management at the next staff meeting. In addition, my client will invite several members of his team to support the project with data gathering.
Time schedule	Name the starting date, any intermediate mileposts, and completion date. If you want to make a progress report for your client, mention this at the kick-off meeting or at the start of your project in addition to including it in the contract.	I can begin work as soon as the contract is signed, which I estimate to be within two weeks. From the start of the project, it will take me two months to complete the project.
Confidentiality	Name who gets what report, because you are almost always dealing with a political situation as well as a technical one.	I will give the results of the project to my client and six members of his senior management.
Client's feedback	Optional: Ask the client to let you know the results of your problem resolution six months after you've completed the project. Seldom do you get feedback but you can ask for it.	I will contact the client for feedback about six months after I've completed the project, either by mailing a written questionnaire or talking to the client by phone.

* *Proposal Guide for Business Development and Sales Professionals.* 2001-2003 Shipley Associates, Business Development Services, Farmington, UT.

PURPOSE OF KICK-OFF MEETINGS

The purpose of a kick-off meeting* is to officially mark the beginning of your engagement, to clearly reestablish the objectives of the work you are assigned to do, and the roles and responsibilities of the people attending the meeting and participating in the project. The meeting should be attended by representatives of the client's management, the people who will benefit from the results of the engagement, and those who will participate in the project. Although all the key people should attend, as with any meeting, keep the size of the meeting small enough to make each person feel that his or her presence is important.

Because the kick-off meeting plays a key role in establishing the tempo of your project, plan carefully to cover the important points of the project such as:

- reviewing the engagement proposal;
- discussing the work objectives;
- defining milestone points in the engagement;
- establishing project completion dates;
- ascertaining client participation in the project.

Before deciding on the details of the kick-off meeting(s), observe these customary rules for planning and scheduling meetings:

- Choose a time convenient for the largest number of participants.
- Schedule a meeting room, either at your office or the client's conference room, that is large enough for the number of participants and is well equipped and away from office disruptions.
- Invite the participants in advance and commit to a completion time for the meeting.
- Prepare an agenda for the meeting and distribute it in advance.

The degree of formality in the meeting agenda may vary, but the basic steps of handling a kick-off meeting remain the same.

Sometime ago, I attended a business simulation of a kick-off meeting, designed for the purpose of teaching consultants about managing the customer engagement process. I learned that the consultant needs to have three things happen to ensure a successful kick-off meeting:

1. Establish rapport or relationship to build trust.
2. Have the client introduce himself or herself first so the people attending the meeting are clear about the purpose of the project and the reason why a consultant is being hired to do the job.
3. Have attendees introduce themselves so they can be comfortable working with you, and you can gain their respect and take advantage of a good opportunity to bond.

Depending on the complexity of the project you are hired for, the kick-off meeting could be a meeting between you and the client, or you and a group of members of the client's organization.

PROGRESS MEETINGS

Whereas the kick-off meeting marks the official start of the project, regular progress meetings are conducted one-on-one. The purpose of progress meetings is to discuss the status of each deliverable, the action items, progress, and any issues.

SAMPLE CONTRACT MODEL

STATE OF VIRGINIA
CONSULTING CONTRACT

Agreement made and entered into this _____ day of _____, _____, by and between _____, a state agency, of
(Name of Agency)

_____, _____, _____,
(Address)   (City)   (State)

_____, (the "State") and _____,
(Zip Code)   (Name)

of _____, _____,
(Company Name)   (Address)

_____, _____, _____,
(City)   (State)   (Zip Code)

_____ (the "Consultant").
(Phone Number)

The State hereby enters into this Agreement for services with Consultant in consideration of and pursuant to the terms and conditions set forth herein.

1. The Consultant will perform those services described in the Work Plan, attached hereto as Exhibit A and by this reference incorporated herein.

2. The Consultant's services under this Agreement shall commence on _____ and end on _____, unless sooner terminated pursuant to the terms hereof.

3. The Consultant will not use State equipment, supplies or facilities.

4. The State will make payment for services upon satisfactory completion of the services. The TOTAL CONTRACT AMOUNT is an amount not to exceed $_____. The State will not pay Consultant's expenses as a separate item. Payment will be made pursuant to itemized invoices submitted with a signed state voucher.

5. The Consultant agrees to indemnify and hold the State of Virginia, its officers, agents and employees, harmless from and against any and all actions, suits, damages, liability or other proceedings that may arise as the result of performing services hereunder. This section does not require the Consultant to be responsible for or defend against claims or damages arising solely from errors or omissions of the State, its officers, agents or employees.

6. The Consultant, at all times during the term of this Agreement, shall obtain and maintain in force insurance coverage of the types and with the limits as follows:

   A. Commercial General Liability Insurance:
   The Consultant shall maintain occurrence based commercial general liability insurance or equivalent form with a limit of not less than $_____ for each occurrence. If such insurance contains a general aggregate limit it shall apply separately to this Agreement or be no less than two times the occurrence limit.

B. Professional Liability Insurance or Miscellaneous Professional Liability Insurance:

The Consultant agrees to procure and maintain professional liability insurance or miscellaneous professional liability insurance with a limit not less than $_____.

C. Business Automobile Liability Insurance:

The Consultant shall maintain business automobile liability insurance or equivalent form with a limit of not less than $_____ for each accident. Such insurance shall include coverage for owned, hired and non-owned vehicles.

D. Worker's Compensation Insurance:

The Consultant shall procure and maintain workers' compensation and employers' liability insurance as required by Virginia law.

Before beginning work under this Agreement, the Consultant shall furnish the State with properly executed Certificates of Insurance which shall clearly evidence all insurance required in this Agreement and which provide that such insurance may not be canceled, except on thirty days' prior written notice to the State. The Consultant shall furnish copies of insurance policies if requested by the State.

7. While performing services hereunder, the Consultant is an independent contractor and not an officer, agent, or employee of the State of Virginia.

8. Consultant agrees to report to the State any event encountered in the course of performance of this Agreement which results in injury to the person or property of third parties, or which may otherwise subject Consultant or the State to liability. Consultant shall report any such event to the State immediately upon discovery.

Consultant's obligation under this section shall only be to report the occurrence of any event to the State and to make any other report provided for by their duties or applicable law. Consultant's obligation to report shall not require disclosure of any information subject to privilege or confidentiality under law (e.g., attorney-client communications). Reporting to the State under this section shall not excuse or satisfy any obligation of Consultant to report any event to law enforcement or other entities under the requirements of any applicable law.

9. This Agreement may be terminated by either party hereto upon thirty (30) days written notice. In the event the Consultant breaches any of the terms or conditions hereof, this Agreement may be terminated by the State at any time with or without notice. If termination for such a default is effected by the State, any payments due to Consultant at the time of termination may be adjusted to cover any additional costs to the State because of Consultant's default. Upon termination, the State may take over the work and may award another party an agreement to complete the work under this Agreement. If after the State terminates for a default by Consultant it is determined that Consultant was not at fault, then the Consultant shall be paid for eligible services rendered and expenses incurred up to the date of termination.

10. This Agreement depends upon the continued availability of appropriated funds and expenditure authority from the Legislature for this purpose. If for any reason the Legislature fails to appropriate funds or grant expenditure authority, or funds become unavailable by operation of law or federal funds reductions, this Agreement will be terminated by the State. Termination for any of these reasons is not a default by the State nor does it give rise to a claim against the State.

11. This Agreement may not be assigned without the express prior written consent of the State. This Agreement may not be amended except in writing, which writing shall be expressly identified as a part hereof, and be signed by an authorized representative of each of the parties hereto.

12. This Agreement shall be governed by and construed in accordance with the laws of the State of Virginia. Any lawsuit pertaining to or affecting this Agreement shall be venued in Circuit Court, Sixth Judicial Circuit, Loudoun County, Virginia.

13. The Consultant will comply with all federal, state and local laws, regulations, ordinances, guidelines, permits and requirements applicable to providing services pursuant to this Agreement, and

will be solely responsible for obtaining current information on such requirements.

14. The Consultant may not use subcontractors to perform the services described herein without the express prior written consent of the State. The Consultant will include provisions in its subcontracts requiring its subcontractors to comply with the applicable provisions of this Agreement, to indemnify the State, and to provide insurance coverage for the benefit of the State in a manner consistent with this Agreement. The Consultant will cause its subcontractors, agents, and employees to comply, with applicable federal, state and local laws, regulations, ordinances, guidelines, permits and requirements and will adopt such review and inspection procedures as are necessary to assure such compliance.

15. Any notice or other communication required under this Agreement shall be in writing and sent to the address set forth above. Notices shall be given by and to _____ on behalf of the State, and by _____, on behalf of the Consultant, or such authorized designees as either party may from time to time designate in writing. Notices or communications to or between the parties shall be deemed to have been delivered when mailed by first class mail, provided that notice of default or termination shall be sent by registered or certified mail, or, if personally delivered, when received by such party.

16. In the event that any court of competent jurisdiction shall hold any provision of this Agreement unenforceable or invalid, such holding shall not invalidate or render unenforceable any other provision hereof.

17. All other prior discussions, communications and representations concerning the subject matter of this Agreement are superseded by the terms of this Agreement, and except as specifically provided herein, this Agreement constitutes the entire agreement with respect to the subject matter hereof.

In Witness Whereof, the parties signify their agreement effective the date above first written by the signatures affixed below.

STATE   CONSULTANT

BY:_____   BY: _____

      (NAME)   (NAME)

_____   _____

  (TITLE AND AGENCY)   (TITLE)

_____   _____

      (DATE)   (DATE)

MOST COMMON CONTRACTS

PURCHASE ORDERS

If you consult with larger organizations or the government, purchase orders are a regular part of written contracts. It is a written offer to purchase your services for a specified amount of money. A purchase order is technically considered a one-sided contract, that is, you accept the offer not in writing, but through your performance of the requested service on delivery of the requested product or service. A purchase order can be a two-sided contract when the client and consultant sign it before performance begins. Both types of purchase orders are valid contracts.

SIMPLE CONTRACTS

Normally one or two pages long is an appropriate length for the kind of work that most consultants do. They are easy to interpret and are not intimidating to most people. If you happen to wind up in court, a judge can easily interpret the terms and conditions and make decisions quickly. Consultants normally use simple contracts that contain all the basic information needed for most consulting situations. See example below.

SAMPLE SIMPLE CONTRACT

Agreement for Consultant Service

Client's name and address:

_____

Description of service to be provided to client:

_____

_____

_____

Start date: _____ Completion date: _____

Fees: $ _____ per _____ (hour/day/other).

Total estimated hours/days/other: $ _____

Other costs: $ _____ for

_____

Payment terms: _____

Additional terms and conditions, if any:

_____

_____

For _____ (consultant) _____ (client)

_____ (signed)   _____ (signed)

_____ (date)   _____ (date)

COMPLEX CONTRACTS

In addition to the terms and conditions contained in simple contracts, complex contracts contain additional terms of conditions meant to address any and every problem or legal challenge that could possibly occur during the course of project performance and beyond. You'll add entire paragraphs or pages on titles such as warranties, terminations, governing law, force majeure (events or conditions beyond the control of either party that interferes with delivery of service and project completion such as natural disasters and fire), and much more. Unless you have experience with the terms and conditions normally contained in complex contracts, you may need to seek an advice from a good lawyer when you are confronted with long and complex contracts. Read all new contracts very thoroughly to make you understand what is expected of you.

KEY POINTS

- Gather the facts that are needed to include in a contract.
- Know how to define a contract.
- Understand what makes a valid contract.

- Understand why you need a written contract.
- Know the elements of a contract.
- Know the purpose of kick-off and progress meetings.
- Determine when to use simple and complex contracts and understand elements needed in each.

Chapter Fourteen
Preparing Reports and Presentations

I write as straight as I can, just as I walk as straight as I can, best that is the best way to get there.
— **H.G. Wells**

Preparing reports and presentations takes a lot of thought, time, and effort. You need to gather information from people involved in your projects, including your clients.

A report is a document containing information organized in a narrative, graphic, or tabular form.

WRITING AND PRESENTING YOUR PROGRESS REPORT

Most consulting projects need to produce, at minimum, a written report, and often deliverables, such as software, tapes, slides, or manuals. If the project is large or long-term, you will probably be required to submit periodic progress or interim reports in addition to a final report. Progress or interim reports allow the client to monitor the status of your project, judge its progress, and learn of any problems or issues.

Progress and interim reports are usually prepared on a regular basis, such as monthly. This kind of reporting benefits both you and your client by providing each of you with an ongoing account of your progress toward meeting your client's objectives. Each report serves as a checkpoint that enables you to make any necessary adjustments if the project is not proceeding as planned. Such reports also increase the chances that the consultant will be successful and the client satisfied. Progress or interim reports are usually presented as a continuing series. Your report should be linked with your prior month's report, if done monthly, which is helpful when you are measuring progress. The content of a progress report covers specific problems, solutions, and plans for solving the problems in the month to come.

How do progress or interim reports look? They can be long narrative pieces, containing visual or graphic material, memos, and letters, or they can be short, one-page memoranda. Longer reports are generally required as part of government contracts and are also appropriate in situations where large capital expenses are involved.

Shorter reports—generally about four pages long—are used in most cases. They take relatively little effort to prepare. I write reports and presentations all the time. The content varies, depending on the project. Typically, I write a preliminary report "zeroing-in" on key findings when I first get some data that I find useful to the client. My purpose in doing a preliminary report is to get a sense of how the client perceives the project's progress and to establish whether we are getting the information we want. I do not necessarily do the same progress reports as outlined in other consulting books. My reports are simple, in the format of an executive summary.

Table 19. Benefits of a Progress Report

To the Client	To the Consultant
Appreciates being kept informed.	Allows you to keep track and keep yourself and the client informed.
Feels satisfied that consultant's work is making progress and is aligned with mutually established goals.	Acts as procedural guide and continuing reference throughout the project.
Increases client involvement, acceptance, and gratitude.	Provides you with satisfaction that you are fulfilling your tasks.
Is encouraged to use consultant's services in the future while learning more about consultant's methods, findings, and recommendations.	Gives you the opportunity to be rehired for another project with the same company.
Is provided with written proof of what the client has requested and what consultant has done.	Proves that you are a good listener.

Table 20 Components of a Progress Report

Component	Description
Table of Contents	Allows the client to visualize the report's content and organization, to find needed information quickly, and to scan the scope of the data included.
Executive Summary	Is the condensation of the report's structure and content. This is particularly helpful when more than one person receives the report. Upper management usually needs only summary data, while others may want details.
Project background	Is a short history of the project, which helps the client place the project into perspective.
Data-gathering methods	Describes the way you will conduct your work as clearly as possible. Be sure to gear your language to your client.
Analysis and synthesis	Presents the relevant data gathered to date concerning the project and gives a preliminary interpretation of the data.
Findings and conclusions	Identifies what has been learned to date in carrying out the project in relation to the identified objectives.
Recommendations	Corresponds to both the project's objectives and your findings. You identify what needs to be done to achieve those objectives.
Projected or realized benefits	Highlights the benefits achieved thus far in the project. Also lists those that can be achieved through the consultant's recommendations.
Implementation guide	Considers methods for implementing the proposed solution(s).
Appendices	Includes necessary charts, exhibits, tables, and analyses.

WRITING AND PRESENTING YOUR FINAL REPORT

A final report shows your accomplishments, problems, plans, and projections. These have to be lucid, complete, informative, and accurate. They must also be dignified and discreet, and factual in tone and style. The tone must definitely be upbeat, reflecting your confidence in the outcome and specifics of your project.

The final report is an important element in more than one-half of all consulting projects. If you decide to write a final report or write one because the client requires it, these are your next steps:

- Select the appropriate type of report;
- Set the structure and content of the report;
- Decide on the style of the report;
- Prepare, present, and distribute the completed final report.

161

Your decision to prepare a final report, in whatever format you choose, should be based on the benefits for both client and you. If both of you think that it's worth the time and effort to have you prepare one, then write it. If you decide you do not need to prepare a final report, an oral presentation is your other option.

Table 21. Benefits of a Final Report

For Client	For Consultant
Provides written proof that the project has been carried out.	Determines whether the client will carry out your ideas and recommendations based on how effectively you communicate.
Documents consultant's findings, conclusions, and recommendations.	Provides you with a written endorsement (testimonial), which you can use as part of your portfolio.
Provides the only systematic presentation of the data, analysis, and findings from consultant's work.	Demonstrates the quality (in its comprehensiveness and clarity) of your output.
Disseminates consultant's ideas and results.	Leads to potential implementation of your ideas, which may result in repeat business.
Demonstrates consultant's successes to upper management, the client, and client's colleagues.	Reminds you of your contributions and achievements.

EXAMPLES OF REPORTS

Annual reports are yearly records of publicly-held companies' financial condition. They summarize the business climate, company operational results, and projections for the following year.

Business reports are documents that present data and information to specific readers. They present pertinent facts, figures, and information for analysis to allow companies to create business plans and budgets, and make marketing and advertising decisions.

CREATING PRESENTATIONS

A presentation is a formal delivery of information. Creating attractive visuals is a sign of professionalism. Visual aids help your client(s) grasp information quickly, provide a change of pace, add interest, lessen your reliance on your words alone, and transfer attention from you to the visuals to relieve you of unnecessary stress. You can use PowerPoint software to create your slides, selecting bullets as a format to list your key messages. You can then expand on each key message orally. Always prepare before you present. Even when you know your subject, if you are not comfortable speaking in front of people, you need preparation time. Presentations to clients are rarely spontaneous, because you are presenting facts. Know your subject thoroughly, use an outline to plan an organized sequence of information, don't look down too much to read your notes, and try to anticipate questions ahead of time.

Always make a presentation for a large project, and do so for smaller projects on a case-by-case basis. If your client insists on a presentation for a small project, make it informal. A meeting with your client should suffice.

As a member of Toastmasters International, I had experience making impromptu presentations within a limited time period of two to five minutes. Presentations on topics are given to you without warning, and you are expected to think fast on your feet, organize your ideas logically and sequentially, and use a variety of presentation techniques to ensure that your audience listens to what you are saying.

Here are some techniques that I learned from attending Toastmaster's International presentation skills course:

- Relax. Don't exhibit jittery behaviors, such as jingling the coins in your pocket, twisting around, and not looking audience members in the eye.
- Be optimistic and enthusiastic. Listening to a presenter who speaks with gusto makes an audience equally optimistic, enthusiastic, and interested in what is being said.
- Speak loudly and slowly. Do not whisper or hold your hand over your mouth. Pronounce your words well, especially if you are not a native speaker of English, because your accent may throw the audience off. You can tell disinterest or confusion when you see people yawning, doodling, or looking at the ceiling.
- Use an outline. You can write your outline on an index card, notepad, or a visual aid the the audience can follow, but don't read your notes. Merely glance at your outline to see where you are in your presentation.

- Vary your sentence length. Have some short, and some long sentences.
- Avoid non-words. Become aware of any habit you may have of saying "ah," "um," or "y'know" when you are presenting. Such habits are distracting to the listener.
- Use a conversational tone to avoid sounding monotonous. Vary your tone by adding emphasis to parts of your message.
- Vary your pace and volume so your audience will pay attention. Go faster or slower for different parts of your message, depending on what you are saying. Pay attention to your voice. Are you speaking too soft? Too loud?
- Use gestures for emphasis. Gestures, like pointing to a visual or a picture, make you look relaxed and natural and give your listeners visual variety. Pause every now and then if you are moving on to another topic to let the audience grasp the shift in subject.
- Be aware of your body language. Experienced presenters know when and how to move their faces, their eyes, and their feet. You do not want to stand in one position throughout your presentation.
- Maintain eye contact. Look people in the eye when you are talking. This doesn't mean concentrating on one person. You can look at each person, but always look him or her straight in the eye and hold for a few moments so you don't appear to be hopping all over the room.
- Have proper posture. Don't slouch or drape yourself across the lectern. Like hand gestures, proper posture is key to looking comfortable, appearing confident, and presenting well.
- Use visual aids effectively. Don't turn your back on your audience to speak to the blackboard or screen. Make visuals bright and colorful, able to be seen with some of the lights on so that you can be seen as well. A dark room encourages snoozing.
- Stop on time. The time you spend depends on the volume of information you need to present. Be sure to plan accordingly and let your client know the length of your presentation in advance.

PRESENTING YOUR FINAL OUTPUT IN OTHER MEDIA

Chances are you might not be limited to presenting a written report or an oral presentation. Your client might also ask you to provide your output in different media: instructional materials, manuals, audio-visuals, program tapes, designs, drawings, specifications, and administrative guidelines.

You have to clearly understand your client's expectations before putting your energy into a specific medium that your client may find unacceptable or inadequate. Get your client's approval before you present your final output, you want to avoid creating a problem and souring your relationship. Anticipating alternatives and seeking client preferences shows your professionalism and experience. If you are using visuals, make sure to convert a mass of text and numbers into simple graphs and charts.

When presenting, you can also use other kinds of visual aids, such as:

- Handouts: Printed information with both text and graphics.
- Whiteboards/Chalkboards: Ideal for a smaller group, up to thirty people and used to jot down main points of the presentation.
- Flipcharts: Charts consisting of sheets hinged at the top that can be flipped over to present information sequentially. Also good for small groups of up to thirty people. The advantage of using flipcharts is that you can prepare these before the start of the presentation.
- PowerPoint: A Microsoft Office product that provides users with an interface to design multimedia slides to be displayed on your laptop computer and project the presentation onto a full-size projection screen.

KEY POINTS

- Know how to write and present reports.
- Understand the components and benefits of reports.
- Know how to create powerful presentations.
- Describe what you're trying to accomplish in your presentation.

- Create attractive visuals for your presentation that use large font size text and color to improve professionalism and readability.
- Outline major points of your presentation that you want to communicate to your audience.
- Ensure that your introduction and conclusion provide a brief overview of your presentation and sell the audience on the importance of the presentation.
- Ensure that your conclusion revisits your key points, reminding the audience why your presentation is important to them, and leaving your audience feeling energized and inspired.
- Have prepared notes as a backup in case you lose your place in your presentation.
- Bring in reinforcement if necessary, such as other project members especially if the project is highly technical. These project members can address specific aspects of your recommendations and solutions.
- Run through your presentation a couple of times prior to presenting.

Chapter Fifteen
Business Ethics in Consulting

"There is no such thing as business ethics. There's only one kind—you have to adhere to the highest standards."
—**Marvin Bowen, former managing partner of McKinney and Company**

Business ethics are an important element in all businesses, including consulting. Why? Ethics give you the guidelines on how to behave professionally in a given environment. You want to adhere to a professional code of ethics because you want to work with the same client again. Look at your consulting services as repeat businesses—not one-time propositions.

BUSINESS ETHICS DEFINED
Business ethics refers knowing what is right or wrong in the workplace and doing what is right.

Each company has its own "culture." To make matters more challenging, some companies have no defined culture and are in a continual state of change even as they attempt to define their culture. Some, regrettably, are not concerned with their corporate culture—only with the bottom line.

All professions have codes of ethics, consulting included. A sense of ethics distinguishes professional consultants from non-professionals, and protects both you and your clients from non-professional behavior. As a consultant, you have to be trustworthy to inspire confidence in your clients. Your image and reputation as a consultant are among your most valuable assets; you must guard them carefully. Consultants are neither organized nor licensed. There are no fixed codes of honor and no set of standards, rules, or regulations to which they must conform. As a consultant, you have to stick to your own moral strictures. For example, many companies protect confidential information by having consultants sign a non-disclosure agreement before they can start working on a project.

It's a good idea to build your own code of ethics that you can follow, and most consultants use the following:

1. Make realistic promises that you can live up to whether your promises are made orally, in writing, or as part of your proposal.
2. Respect the confidentiality of every client's proprietary information as well as the details of the business relationship between you and your client.
3. Make a strict accounting of your work, what the contract calls for, and what you have completed.
4. Define everything you promise your client.
5. Give your honest opinion.
6. Refrain from recommending services that clients don't need.
7. Disclose conflicts of interest.
8. Conduct yourself with professionalism at all times.

HANDLING ETHICAL MATTERS

The lines between right and wrong and good and bad aren't always clear-cut. What if you're asked to do something that goes against your personal beliefs? What if you have information that one of your clients needs to know, such as when a competitor is bringing out a similar product, but the information was given to you in confidence? What if you stand to gain from the outcome of a recommendation that you make to clients?

The decision to tell or not tell, to do a task or not do it, to make a recommendation or not—all, can involve much soul-searching. In your role as a consultant, you'll be faced with a number of situations where you must decide whether "to do or not to do" something, based on your honesty and integrity in representing your client's best interests within the bounds of what is right.

There are laws and regulations that apply to business ethics, but most of the time, you have to rely solely on your personal judgment to determine the path to take in each and every situation. The best way to keep ethical molehills from becoming mountains is to develop a personal code of behavior to guide your actions and enhance your decision-making ability. Rather than resorting to fire-fighting and crisis-management every time an ethical question arises, you can follow your already established guidelines. Develop your code of ethics early in your consulting career; keep reviewing and modifying it to reflect current views and changes in circumstances.

Sample Code of Consultant's Business Ethics

The basic responsibility of every consultant is to put the interest of clients ahead of personal interests, and to serve clients with integrity and competence.

- I know that I am being hired for my independent judgment and objectivity, technical expertise, analytical skills, and concentrated attention to resolving an identified problem.
- I will respect the confidentiality of all clients' information. I will not take financial gain or any other kind of advantage based on inside information. I will not work on sensitive problems for two or more competing clients without obtaining the approval of each client. I shall inform clients of any circumstances that might influence my judgment or objectivity.
- I will confer with a client in sufficient detail before accepting an assignment to understand the problem and scope of study needed to solve the problem. I shall bear in mind that preliminary consultations are conducted confidentially, even though terms have not yet been agreed to and a contract might never result.
- I shall accept only those assignments I am qualified to perform. I shall not guarantee specific results, such as amount of cost reduction or profit increase. I shall present my qualifications on the basis of my competence and experience. I shall perform each assignment on an individualized basis and develop customized

recommendations for the practical solution of each client's problem.

- I shall establish in advance my agreement with clients on the fee basis for an assignment.
- I shall make sure the client understands what work is included and what work carries an additional fee.

Exercise 5
Handling Business Ethics Case Studies

Instructions: Read Case Study 1 and write your responses in the space provided. Then do the same with Case Study 2. Once you have completed both case studies, turn to the next page to see the suggested solutions.

Case Study 1

During the course of your project assignment, you discover illegal payments and other questionable management practices. Your client is a large publicly held company. After your discovery, you make this observation to an employee:

I am here as a consultant handling confidential information although my client is open in telling me information I should not be privy to.

Do you have the obligation to tell your client what is right and wrong? Do you have to be policing what your client tells you? What response should you make to your comment?

Your solution?

_____

_____

_____

Case Study 2

You have completed and submitted your final report to your client. There are no punches in your final report, but you found it difficult to be objective in your findings, conclusions, and recommendations. What should you do?

<u>Your solution?</u>

_____

_____

_____

Exercise 5a
Case Study Solutions

Handling Business Ethics Case Studies

Case Study 1 Solution

Non-disclosure is not considered an acceptable alternative because it makes you an accessory to an illegal act. Disclosure to your client only—with no action—may result in the destruction of part of the evidence. Probably, the first step is to report the matter to your client's boss. Circumstances, however, may require that the consultant refer the matter to the client's legal counsel.

Case Study 2 Solution

Professional ethics require your honesty, integrity, and responsibility to place your personal interests ahead of the client's interests. You wrote the final report based on the available facts.

LOOKING AT COMMON ETHICAL ISSUES AND DISCUSSION OF SOLUTIONS

Issue 1: Practices that are clearly unethical or illegal.

Discussion of solution 1: Be sure you understand the background. Find out more before you step up to the issue. These issues are "land mines" that will, once identified, make the organization and your client vulnerable. Protect yourself and your client by confidentially addressing the matter with the CEO. Do so with insight into how the issue might be mitigated or fully resolved. A good consultant can stop a crisis before it begins.

Issue 2: Conflicts of interest (competing interests that can interfere with your obligations to various people and organizations).

Discussion of solution 2: Your client may have a contracting officer who maintains a history of various contracting firms and subcontractors. Although your client confides in you, be aware of the sensitivity of the information you are given, which may be proprietary and inappropriate for your consumption to begin with.

Issue 3: Potential pitfalls. Consultants are often asked to assist in writing statements of work and requests for proposals upon which other contractors will bid. Although the client may need your help in getting these requests written, this is not a sanctioned activity. What do you do? Be sure you know what you can do, to what degree you can do it, and in what position it puts you and your client. How does the consultant handle this?

Discussion of solution 3: Ask the contracting officer at the company you are working for (either the client directly, or the prime vendor, if you are a subcontractor) to tell you about the potential pitfalls that you hope to avoid. Both you and the client will be better served by you becoming a well-informed consultant. Look out after your business interests by paying attention to such matters.

KEY POINTS

- As a consultant, no matter your background or the environment where you work, you must decide what is right and wrong, and what practices you are willing to perform on behalf of your client.
- Each type of consulting arrangement has its own ethical implications. Honesty IS the best policy. You, more than anyone else, must be impeccable in the way you conduct business. Proprietary information or sensitive matters must be kept absolutely confidential. Your ability to be discreet, professional, tactful, and diplomatic will be appreciated and duly noted. In the long run, this ability will bolster your professional reputation. And in the short run, it keeps you out of the "dog fights" that can occur.
- Buy into the practice of NOT talking about others and not keeping a secret by "telling only one person at a time." You will be faced with countless opportunities to weigh in, give advice, and counsel. You are, after all, a consultant, and a confidante to

someone about something. But you need to know where you fit, to lead by example, and to give your client the best advice on how to do the same.

- Maintain access, time, arms-length objectivity, and an implied mandate to make your client and his or her organization better. When complex matters require thorough analysis, don't bring preconceived notions or pat formulas to the table. Gut reactions may or may not be correct and rarely demonstrate a diligent process of study and analysis. However, do not fail to observe and address—if appropriate—matters of illegality or questionable ethical behavior with your client. Your client may not be fully aware of the existence or the impact of certain issues, which bring vulnerability, morale problems, and legal culpability to his or her doorstep.

Chapter Sixteen
Achieving Success in Consulting

The key to success is setting aside eight hours a day for work and eight hours of sleep and making sure they're not the same hours.
—John D. Rockefeller, Jr.

Success is a combination of having fun, making a difference, making your passion your life's work, and more. Success is what you need to make you feel happy and fulfilled. If you can achieve your needs and most of your goals while also making a difference, making money, and meeting or exceeding your personal and professional objectives, then you are successful!

CONSULTING SUCCESS DEFINED

Success is a state of mind. It is not a singular or rare event or a pot of gold at the end of the rainbow. Success is a personal matter, subject to your own definition. You live in a materialistic society in which some folks equate success with worth, power, and prestige—whatever trappings they think of as evidence of wealth. This is not what success is about.

Consulting success doesn't happen by accident or by chance. You achieve success through ambition, clear goals, hard work, motivation, patience, persistence, planning, research, and support from others. In the consulting business, all other indicators of success are hollow if you are unable to earn enough to pay your bills and provide yourself with an acceptable salary. In this business, you have to define success as success in the marketplace; that is, selling whatever you offer as a consultant.

Consulting is not a "one-call business." You rarely win a client and an assignment immediately after an initial sales call. Potential clients usually buy consulting services much as they do a car: after extensive shopping, several inquiries, and some comparative evaluations. Like a car salesman, you must also woo and win your client. You have to continuously market your services because even word-of-mouth referrals do not always bring hordes of other clients knocking on your door the moment you complete an assignment. Even the most successful marketing may only result in a work assignment after many months of persistent effort.

MOST COMMON PITFALLS IN CONSULTING

Success, especially in your first year of consulting, does not come easily. Because consulting is like any other business, a consultancy is not exempt from the highs and lows.

PITFALLS CAN BE ATTRIBUTED TO:

- **Over-selling and under-delivering.** If one thing irks clients, it is consultants promising more than they can deliver. New consultants are tempted to be overeager—the same feeling you have when you get your very first job. You want to get going and prove yourself, perhaps underestimating the work involved. Over eagerness can hurt more than help you. Ultimately you may lose clients because of promising too much.
- **Poor listening skills.** Consultants' skills depend upon listening attentively to what clients are saying. Because you are there to meet their needs, make sure you know exactly what they are asking of you. If you are distracted and fail to capture all the requirements, you will surely go a different route than the clients require (or intend).

- **Building a business, not a relationship.** Consulting is a people business, and building rapport with clients is invaluable. Always treat your clients well; they do not forget bad relationships.
- **Inadequate marketing.** Marketing is a priority for selling your services. Even if you have signed contracts from a few clients, you should continue your marketing efforts. If you stop marketing yourself, you will find out one day that your projects are ending and your client base is drying up. By the time you realize this, and find your next job, you might experience considerable down time.
- **Lack of business skills.** Consulting is a business and has to be run like one. Doing your consulting work is only one half of the equation. The other half of the business requires you to balance your accounts, pay your bills, reconcile your taxes, sign and negotiate your lease (if you are renting office space), monitor your overhead expenses, and check your cash flow.
- **Lack of capital.** It is very easy to underestimate the money you need to launch your consulting business and keep it going. Because the first year may not yield profits, you need a cash reserve for ongoing expenses.
- **Importance of signed proposals.** Proposals are more than selling tools; they are good communication tools that help eliminate misunderstandings. They are also mini-contracts that protect both client and you, important documents that both parties should agree to and sign. They keep your project assignment and relationship on track.
- **Poor communication.** Too little or no communication spells disaster. Nothing is too small or too unimportant to report to the client; you are better off over-communicating than under-communicating. Failing to communicate with your client regularly might cost you later on in the project. Clients want to be informed about the progress of the project. You don't have to use an elaborate means to communicate with them; you can send notes weekly, make a telephone call weekly, or provide a written addendum or weekly invoice. The more you inform the client, the smoother the project will progress. There is no such thing as too much information.

- **Uncertainty about billing.** Billing is related to communication. Avoid surprising your client with an expense that you have not explained nor provided back-up receipts for. Even with mutual trust, establish a policy of providing detailed expense reports that allow your client to verify your expenditures.

Can any of these pitfalls be remedied? Absolutely! If you are aware that they exist, you can find ways to fix them.

TURNING PITFALLS INTO CONSULTING SUCCESS

NINE STEPS TO FOLLOW TO ACHIEVE SUCCESS:

1. **Remain committed.** Commitment is the #1 success ingredient. A full commitment to pursuing a consulting career is absolutely essential. It is easy to get discouraged. At times, the gaps between assignments can seem long. Use the time between assignments to market your services as never before, and invest some time in personal development.
2. **Focus on clients' needs.** What you believe you can do for your clients is not nearly as important as knowing what they actually need. Taking extra time upfront to assess clients' needs in-depth can make a major difference in the perceived quality of the results you deliver.
3. **Develop your own unique selling proposition.** Come up with a compelling two-minute sales pitch. Being able to clearly and concisely articulate your product and services helps you position yourself in a client's mind. That edge gives you the opportunity to step up and explain, during face-to-face or telephone meetings, why your services should be considered.
4. **Have financial reserves available.** Make sure you have enough money to cover your business expenses. Also plan for unexpected expenses and the need to maintain a steady cash flow. Know from the start that your net ten-day payment terms do not necessarily mean that all clients will pay in ten days. Consider all operational

costs when calculating your expense rate. Business plans do not always cover all the bases.

5. **Develop and expand your contacts.** As mentioned above in the business skills section, consulting is a people business. The more you can tap into newly developed contacts, the faster your business will grow. These contacts may be able to use your services directly, but if not, they can at least provide valuable referrals. The degree of success you have in your first year in consulting will depend upon the number of quality business contacts you make. When you start your business, your success beyond the start-up period will depend heavily on your ability to continually establish new contacts.

6. **Spread the word.** Word-of-mouth is a fast and effective marketing tool; it is free publicity. Also consider publishing a newsletter that you can give to existing or potential clients. You can also publish a newsletter on the web on a quarterly basis.

7. **Focus on results.** Results are the driving force motivating potential clients to use your services. Consulting has changed from being an advice profession to one focused on producing results for clients.

8. **Get testimonials.** Take the time to collect written endorsements from clients you worked with or people who know about you and your consulting business. Because of the business's people-centered nature and the importance of credibility and trust, make the effort to ask for quotations, testimonial letters, and referrals from each client. What someone else says about you is far more important than anything you can say about yourself. Proactively ask your clients to write to you and tell you that they were satisfied with your services and why. Written, quotable comments make credibility issues go away when talking with new clients.

9. **Provide more value than expected.** Any extra efforts you provide your clients can only benefit you in the future, and this helps to create a bond between you and your clients.

KEY POINTS

- Know what you want, where you want it, when you want it, and how much money you need or want for it.
- Bring your special talents to clients who have a need for them; perform the work in a place and over a period of time that meets your needs and the client's; and be well compensated and respected.
- Bring your good attitude, strong skills, experience, and professionalism to the table. You will succeed, make a difference, and have one hell of a good life doing it as a consultant.

Conclusion

Starting Your Career as a Consultant gives you the basics before you go into consulting as well as practices and trends in the profession. As you become more experienced, many other books are available that you can use to enhance your knowledge about consulting.

The demands you face now will not be the same demands as in the future. Look at your new career as a starting point and continue to persevere. Later, you will have opportunities to expand your operations and work competitively with more experienced consultants.

Consulting is a people business. In earlier years, a consultant's primary role was to provide advice and counsel. That role is changing now. Clients are looking for more than advice. They are looking for people who can provide innovative solutions to complex problems, can handle business functions (marketing, accounting, invoicing, management, and administration), and can plan and think strategically. If you used the tools in this book to rate your personal attributes to see if you fit the mold of a consultant, and if you completed the self-assessment exercise and various personality tests, your results will help determine whether consulting is the profession for you. You need a variety of skills to make it: technical, managerial/administrative, and entrepreneurial. In most cases, you need to be an entrepreneur first because this skill is the main driver for your future as a consultant.

If you look closely at yourself and the consulting business in a broader context, you can see that consultants share many common traits. However, none is more evident than a positive outlook.

Although success is your ultimate goal, you don't get there without crossing humps and rebounding from the bumps. You will experience some struggles, challenges, and mistakes. These are part of the learning process. It is important to do well with a first client so you can get recommendations to others. Once you achieve that, a letter of appreciation or commendation from the client will give you the confidence you need as you continue to market yourself and work with others.

The current trends of downsizing, acquisitions, and mergers will continue, meaning continuing demands for consultants. If you are a generalist (a "Jack of all trades"), you will have to learn to be a specialist. Why? Clients are looking for expertise in technology and strategy planning. With new industries continuing to develop locally and globally, the demand for consultants of all kinds and specialties will continue to increase significantly.

Consultants and the consulting business will keep changing. If you are working solo now, you might have to look at joining "consulting networks." These consulting networks are set up either formally or informally, and they are designed to serve very specific needs, such as the need for expertise in specialized technologies and geographical distribution.

The impact of such changes is to make competition keener, even cutthroat, and to necessitate your developing niche markets requiring specialized skills. As the need for specialists grows, you will have to acquire different skills, arts, and technologies to solve your clients' complex problems and needs. Even as a new consultant, be prepared to do and learn more. How will the future look for you? The future is now. You may have to be more flexible and adaptable, and work harder. You may need to wear several new hats.

To prepare yourself for the future, here are some practical tips you may want to consider:

- Work individually or form alliances with "networkers."
- Diversify your specializations into niche markets that you develop from your own expertise.
- Follow your clients into foreign markets, which are expanding because of globalization, although this is a choice you need to make based on your desire and situation.

- Become more competitive and develop new promotional or marketing techniques, such as making greater use of a combination of traditional marketing (e.g., paper-based advertising) and social media marketing platforms (e.g., Facebook, LinkedIn, Twitter, blogs).
- Become more resourceful and innovative. With the trend toward strategic planning and innovative solutions, be constantly aware of market trends and examine them closely.
- Know how to conceptualize and become comfortable with unique or eclectic client needs.
- Use different applications to solve problems.
- Because consulting continues to change in very subtle ways, you will have to make changes as the world changes.
- Because the marketplace for consulting itself is being changed in many ways, consultants will become specialists rather than remain generalists. There will be more demand by clients for specialized skills.
- Develop specialized skills needed as a result of advances in communication, information retrieval, and other fields of advanced technology. Technologies are narrowing the gap between client and consultant in access to knowledge. Therefore, consultants need more training in newer technologies to keep ahead of their clients. Attending state-of-the-art training and seminars will become the norm.

In summary, you shouldn't lose sight of your purpose in starting a career in consulting—why you went into the business to begin with—always push forward and aim higher. Don't lose focus. Revisit your purpose—what do you want to achieve and when do you want to achieve it? Continue to check where you are and how far still do you want to go. Continue to practice. Continue to learn and apply what you learn through strategic planning.

Whatever else can be said about consulting, you can guarantee one thing—you won't be bored. Although you are advised to stick to a firm daily schedule, whether you are on assignment or not, it is a solid bet that you will not get bogged down by routine. You will have too much to do, and more variety in your day than you know how to handle. Although you will work hard, the fact is, consulting allows you a high degree of control over your own level of job satisfaction. Not many jobs can promise this. That's why you'll love consulting.

FREQUENTLY ASKED QUESTIONS

Becoming a Consultant: Frequently Asked Questions

Question	Answer
How do I get started as a consultant?	First – identify your areas of expertise. Ask yourself: What services can you provide a potential client? What problems can you solve?
What tax deductions can I take working from a home office?	For starters, you can deduct the space within your home designated as a home office. Two ways to do this: either by the room itself or by square footage. You can also deduct mileage from your home office to wherever you are conducting business with a client; same for entertainment expenses if you meet a prospective client over lunch. Go to www.nolo.com to read article on "What are the deductions for the self-employed."
Is there a downside to becoming a consultant as opposed to continuing to work as an employee?	The short answer is that becoming a consultant is not for everyone and there are always tradeoffs in life. In order to become a consultant, you must be willing to take responsibility for your own work life and finances. In effect, you become a small business and must, for example, pay for your own insurance, control your own retirement plan, and pay the full amount of your Social Security taxes. The tradeoff is that you can also demand a much higher rate of pay. All of this entails learning some things about contracting with businesses for your services, paying your taxes, keeping up with your budget, and a myriad of other things that you don't consider when you are an employee.
What's the biggest problem I will face in consulting?	<ul><li>Knowing what steps to take</li><li>Finding clients</li><li>Setting consulting fees</li><li>Marketing my business</li><li>Business planning</li></ul>

Question	Answer
Before becoming a consultant, do I need special licensing and certification?	Some fields require special license or certificate. Insurance, real estate, financial planning are some of the areas where you need special certification.
In becoming a consultant, do I need to incorporate?	Becoming a consultant doesn't mean you need to start a complex business. You can simply work as a sole proprietor in many places. However, because regulations vary from one jurisdiction to the next, contact your government business agent. Check the Small Business Administration through www.sba.gov.
Does becoming a consultant cost a lot?	Becoming a consultant can cost as little or as much as you want. Some people can become consultants simply by getting a city business permit and handing out their name and number. In Virginia Beach for instance, a city business permit for working from home is $40 yearly. Others need websites, home offices, brochures, licensing, and other materials. By creating a business plan, you can figure out how much it costs before you take the plunge in becoming a consultant.
Is becoming a consultant worth it?	Becoming a consultant is a personal decision. No one else can tell you if you'll enjoy becoming a consultant. However, you can identify characteristics that may help you find your way in becoming a consultant: • Do you like to work regular hours? • Is it important to you to have a steady paycheck? • Are you willing to do your own administrative work, such as answering the phone, photocopying, responding to email, mailing out information, and other tasks that you might currently have other people to help.
How much should I ask for my consulting services?	You should ask for a much higher hourly consulting fee than is provided an hourly wages to employees. Some research into the cost to a company for an employee will

Question	Answer
	provide you with a good guideline. For example, you may ask the company what their overhead costs are for insurance, retirement plans, and taxes and negotiate a consulting fee that will provide you with more of a profit while costing the company less at the same time. If a company pays a professional employee $75/hour in wages and it costs an additional $35/hour in insurance, retirement contributions, and taxes, for a total cost of $110/hour, you should be able to negotiate a consulting fee in that neighborhood, give or take a few dollars. You negotiate with the company to show that you can help to reduce their HR costs, including the administrative cost if they were to hire you as an employee instead of a consultant.
Are you confident about my ability to get the job done? How do I win clients' confidence?	There are seven important attributes of winning client confidence: be ethical, be willing to solve challenges, offer options/don't dictate, bring new perspectives, be a good listener, be a team player, and treat all engagements as special.
How do I build up my confidence?	Confidence will come to you over time. Work on simple projects first. Build up the challenge element in your projects at a pace that you feel comfortable and you will be fine. Constantly educate yourself by reading and networking on consulting methods and case studies.
How do I avoid over commitment?	Common causes of over commitment are when you do not plan your work, you are a procrastinator, and you did not realize the size of the task. Consultants come up with proper proposals that specify exact deliverables, time, cost and conditions. This practice will help you plan your time.
How do I maintain work life balance and reduce stress?	Consulting is not for everyone. You have to be prepared for long hours and intense pressure of deadlines.

Question	Answer
What do I need to do to get new assignments?	To get new assignments, you need to build trust with your client and you will automatically hear about challenges clients are facing. You may have to give some free time upfront in small focus workshops and research work to assist clients in formulating a case. This is purely pre-sales effort. Though consultants don't get paid for this work, the chances of winning such deals are 80% as compared to Request for Proposals (RFPs) that rarely achieves a win rate over 20 percent.
How do I switch context when I am working in multiple projects?	You will always find yourself working in multiple projects as a consultant. Plan upfront. Chart your milestones with clear deliverables and keep documentation and notes. Set up a timetable to work on each project based on your deliverable schedule. Stick to commitments and reach out for help if you find yourself falling behind. Do not work on more than two large engagements or four short ones at a given time.
How do I deal with a difficult client or one who is an expert in their field?	It is true that most clients will possess a high degree of domain knowledge than a consultant who is a starting out professional. Your value is not in domain knowledge but in ability to solve problems and bringing new perspectives.
What are the typical pitfalls in consulting?	Wrong attitude is the number one killer.
What are the signs of a good consultant?	A good consultant is one who is requested by a client for repeat business. To make yourself "in demand," you need to be creative and diligent. In addition, consultants should develop a work style to that of a "trusted advisor." This is a phrase coined by a Harvard Professor David H. Maister. In short, if you are hard working, enthusiastic about solving challenges and complement your clients' capabilities, you will automatically become a good consultant.

Question	Answer
How does a consultant market himself?	Figure out where your strengths lie. Find out what you are really good at and sell that.
How should you set your rates?	Realize that not all work is billable hours. You might work forty or even sixty hours a week, but a good portion of that time will be spent on paperwork, phone calls, and other tasks that you shouldn't bill your clients. If you bill thirty-two hours a week, this is pretty good and you are doing well. Determining the best rates for your work might take some research and some trial and error. If you give a quote and you hear your client groan, but he agrees to pay it, you're at the right amount. If your client says yes too quickly, you are probably setting your fee too low. Setting your fees too late can actually turn some clients off.

KEY BUSINESS, FINANCING, AND MARKETING WEBSITES

Here's a compilation that might be useful to you:

GENERAL SMALL BUSINESS SITES

- All Business
  www.allbusiness.com
  All Business provides articles and expert advice on all areas of business, including business plans.

- American Home Business Association
  www.homebusinessnetworks.com
  American Home Business Association provides practical information and advice to home-based entrepreneurs.

- Business Plans
  www.bplans.com
  Business Plan provides sample business plans and plenty of advice on creating them.

- Business Plans (Center for Business Planning)
  www.businessplans.org
  Business Plans provide information about creating business
  plans, including free templates and samples as well as business
  planning products and services.

- Business Town
  www.businesstown.com
  Business Town provides a section on structuring and writing a
  business plan.

- IDEA Café: The Small Business Channel
  www.businessownersideacafe.com
  IDEA Café is a fun approach to serious business! Get information on start-up financing, business communication, and chat
  with other entrepreneurs.

- The Entrepreneur/Small Business Newsletter
  www.masterlink.com
  The Entrepreneur/Small Business Newsletter is a slick list of
  information and articles on financing, marketing, accounting,
  insurance, and legal issues.

- The Mining Company
  www.miningco.com
  The Mining Company is a guide for resources and links for the
  business rookie.

- National Association of Home-Based Business
  www.usahomebusiness.com
  The National Association of Home-Based Business provides
  home business services ranging from joint marketing to a
  consultant who will diagnose flaws in the marketing plan and
  explain how to correct them.

- National Association of Women Business Owners
  www.nawbo.org
  The National Association of Women Business Owners provides
  an opportunity for members to meet and share best practices.

- SBA Online (U.S. Small Business Administration)
  www.sbaonline.sba.gov
  The SBA Online guides you through all the small business programs, services, and resources available through the SBA.

- Small Business News Online
  www.sbnpub.com
  The Small Business News Online offers solutions to the daily challenges of growing a business. Topics include management, finance, marketing, technology, health care, and personnel.

- Smart Business Supersite
  www.smartbiz.com
  Smart Business Supersite is a "how-to" resource for business and start-ups.

- The Small Business Advisor
  www.isquare.com
  The Small Business Advisor is focused especially on entrepreneurs with a new start-up business—lots of books, special reports, and consulting resources available for the asking.

- Working Solo Online
  www.workingsolo.com
  Working Solo Online is a great place to stop by to ask questions and get answers regarding running a one-person operation.

FINANCING SITES

- America's Business Funding Directory
  www.businessfinance.com
  America's Business Funding Director is a free service designed to help those in need of capital sources find it online.

- Quicken
  www.cashfinder.com
  Quicken saves you time and hassle, particularly the business cash finder, which you could use to get funding. This free service lets you shop online for business loans, credit cards, lines of credit, and leases.

MARKETING SITES

- Guerrilla Marketing Online
  www.gmarketing.com
  Guerilla Marketing Online is a weekly column on marketing strategies, as well as write-ups on other helpful sites for the guerrilla entrepreneur.

- The Internet Marketing Center
  www.marketingtips.com
  The Internet Marketing Center shows you many marketing and promotional tips and tricks and how you can promote your business on the Internet.

USEFUL SOCIAL MEDIA WEBSITES

- Blogger (www.blogger.com/start)

- Bloglines (www.bloglines.com)

- Facebook (www.facebook.com)

- Flickr (www.flickr.com)

- Google Blog Search (http://blogsearch.google.com)

- LinkedIn (www.linkedin.com)

- MySpace (www.myspace.com)

- Podcast Alley (www.podcastalley.com)

- Twitter (https://twitter.com)

- TypePad (www.typepad.com)

- Wikia (www.wikia.com/wiki/Wikia)

- Wordpress (http://wordpress.org)

- YouTube (www.youtube.com)

SUGGESTIONS FOR FURTHER READING

Abrams, Rhonda M. *The Successful Business Plan: Secrets and Strategies.* 3rd edition. Palo Alto, CA: Running 'R' Media (™), 2000.

Abrams, Rhonda M. *The Owner's Manual for Small Business.* Palo Alto: CA: The Planning Shop, 2005.

Barrett, Niall. *Building the Custom Home Office: Projects for the Complete Work Space.* Newton, CT: Tarton Press, 2002.

Beech, Wendy. *Guide to Starting Your Own Business.* New York: John Wiley & Sons, Inc.,1999.

Bell, Chip R. and Leonard Nadler (editors). *Clients and Consultants: Meeting and Exceeding Expectation.* 2nd edition. Houston, TX: Gulf Publishing, 1985.

Benjamin, Susan F. *Instant Messaging for (Almost) Free.* Naperville, IL: Sourcebooks, 2007.

Berrington, John, and Carl Finkbeiner. *Segmentation Marketing.* New York: Harper Business, 1992.

Block, Peter. *Flawless Consulting: A Guide to Getting Your Expertise Used.* 3rd edition. Austin, TX: Learning Concepts, 2011

Bly, Robert W. *Selling Your Services.* New York: Henry Holt, 1991.

Bodnar, Kipp and Jeffrey L. Cohen. *Becoming a Marketing Superstar.* Hoboken, NJ: John Wiley & Sons, Inc., 2012.

Bowie, Norman E. and Meg Schneider. *Business Ethics for Dummies.* Hoboken, NJ: Wiley Publishing, Inc., 2011.

Carter, Brian and Justin Levy. *Facebook Marketing.* 3rd edition. Indianapolis, IN: Que Publishing, 2012.

Cates, Bill. *Get More Referrals Now!* USA: McGraw Hill, 2004.

Chase, Larry. *Internet World - Essential Business Tactics for the Net.* New York: John Wiley & Sons, Inc., 1998.

Chipps, Genie, and Claudia Jessup. *The Woman's Guide to Strategic Business.* 3rd edition. New York: Henry Holt, 1991.

Corello, Joseph A., and Brian J. Hazelgren. *The Complete Book of Business Plans*. Naperville, IL: Sourcebooks, 2005.

Corello, Joseph A., and Brian J. Hazelgren. *Your First Business Plan*. 5th edition. Naperville, IL: Sourcebooks, 2006.

Daum, Kevin and Matt Scott, Bettina Hein and Andreas Goeldi. *Video Marketing for Dummies*. Hoboken, NJ: John Wiley & Sons, Inc., 2012.

Duryee, David A. *The Business Owner's Guide to Achieving Financial Success*. New York: Irwin Professional Publishing, 1994.

Editors of Toolkit Media Group. *Business Plans That Work*. 3rd edition. Riverwoods, IL, 2008.

Emerson, Melinda F. *Become Your Own Boss in 12 Months*. Aron, MA: Adams Media, 2010.

Esar, Evan. *20,000 Quips and Quotes*. New York: Barnes & Noble Books, 1968.

Finch, Brian. *How to Write a Business Plan*. 3rd edition. Philadelphia: Kogan, 2010.

Fishman, Stephen. *Working for Yourself: Law and Taxes for Independent Contractors, Freelancers and Consultants*. 8th edition. Berkeley, CA: Nolo Press, 2011.

Gillin, Paul. *Secrets of Social Media Marketing*. Fresno, CA: Quill Driver Books, 2009.

Gleeson, Kerry. *The Personal Efficiency Program: How to Get Organized to Do More Work in Less Time*. 3rd edition. New York: John Wiley & Sons, Inc., 2004.

Gram, Douglas, BA, LLB. *Start and Run a Consulting Business*. Bellingham, WA: Self-Counsel Press, Ltd., 2010.

Green, Charles H. *Get Financing Now*. New York: McGraw Hill, 2012.

Hargrave, Lee E., Jr. *Plans for Profitability! How to Write a Strategic Business Plan*. Titusville, FL: Four Seasons Publishers, 1999.

Henricks, Mark. *Business Plans Made Easy: It's Not as Hard as You Think!* 2nd edition. Irvine, CA: Entrepreneur Media, Inc., 2002.

Holtz, Herman. *The Concise Guide to Becoming an Independent Consultant.* Canada: John Wiley & Sons, Inc., 1999.

Jolles, Robert L. *How to Run Seminars and Workshops: Presentation Skills for Consultants, Trainers, and Teachers.* New York: John Wiley & Sons, Inc., 1993.

Kerpen, Dave. *Likeable Social Media.* The McGraw Hill Companies, 2011.

Kintler, David. *Independent Consulting: Your Comprehensive Guide to Building Your Own Consulting Business.* Avon, MA: Adams Media, 1998.

Kirkpatrick, David. *The Facebook Effect.* New York: Simon & Schuster Paperbacks, 2012.

Lewin, Marsha D. *The Overnight Consultant.* New York: John Wiley & Sons, Inc., 1995.

Lewis, David and Robert Sharpe. *The Success Factor.* Crown Publishers, 1976.

McGuckin, Frances. *Business for Beginners.* Naperville, IL: Sourcebooks, Inc., 2005.

Miller, Malcolm. *Brainstyles.* New York: Simon and Schuster, 1997.

Miller, Marlane. *Who You Are.* New York: Simon and Schuster, 1997.

Misner, Ivan, Ph.D. with David Alexander and Brian Hilliard. *Networking Like a Pro.* Canada: Entrepreneur Press, 2009.

Moran, Erin and Sue Johnson. *Business Plans Plus.* New York: Alpha, a member of Penguin Group USA, Inc., 2011

Myers-Briggs, Isabel, with Peter B. Myers. *Gifts Differing: Understanding Personality Type.* Palo Alto, California: Davies-Black Publishing, 1995.

Nelson, Bob, and Peter Economy. *Consulting for Dummies.* Forest City, CA: IDG Books Worldwide, 2008.

Nelson, Bob and Peter Economy. *Consulting for Dummies.* 2nd edition. Hoboken, NJ: Wiley Publishing, Inc., 2008.

O'Donnell, Michael. *Writing Business Plans that Get Results*. Chicago, IL: Contemporary Books, 1991.

O'Reilly, Tim and Sarah Milstein. *The Twitter Book*. 2nd edition. Sebastopol, CA: O'Reilly Media, Inc., 2009.

Parker, Catherine. *301 Ways to Use Social Media Marketing to Boost Your Marketing*. New York: McGraw Hill, 2010.

Parker, James O, Attorney At Law. *The Power of the Self-Employed*. 2nd edition. Naperville, IL: Sphinx (An imprint of Sourcebooks), Inc., 2007.

Paulson, Ed. *Starting Your Own Business*. Alpha, a member of Penguin Group USA, Inc., 2012

Peterson, Steven D., PhD, Peter Jaret and Barbara Findlay Schenck. *Business Plans Kit for Dummies*. 3rd edition. Hoboken, NJ: Wiley Publishing, Inc., 2010.

Peterson, Steven D. and Paul Tiffany, Ph.D. *Business Plans for Dummies*. 2nd edition. Hoboken, NJ: Wiley Publishing, Inc., 2005.

Pinson, Linda, and Jerry Jinnett. *Steps to Small Business Start-up*. 4th edition. Chicago, IL: Dearborn, 2000.

Piper, Mike. *Surprisingly Simple: Independent Contractor, Sole Proprietor and LLC Taxes Explained in 100 Pages or Less*. Chicago, IL: Piper Tax Group, 2007.

Sandlin, Eileen Figure. *Start Your Own Consulting Business*. 3rd edition. USA: Entrepreneur Media, Inc., 2010.

Schein, Edgar H. *Process Consultation Revisited: Building the Helping Relationship*. Reading: MA: Addison-Wesley/Longman, 1998.

Scott, David Meerman. *Real-Time Marketing*. Hoboken, NJ: John Wiley & Sons, Inc., 2012.

Serebriakoff, Victor. *Self-scoring Personality Test - Mensa*. New York: Barnes & Noble Books, 1996.

Shefsky, Lloyd. *Entrepreneurs are Made—Not Born*. New York, 1994.

Siber, Lee T. *Self-Promotion for the Creative Person: Get the Word Out About Who You Are and What You Do.* New York: Three Rivers Press (Crown Publishing), 2001.

Sinetar, Marsha. *To Build the Life You Want, Create the Work You Have.* New York: St. Martin's Press, 1995.

Singh, Shiv and Stephanie Diamond. *Social Media Marketing.* Hoboken, NJ: John Wiley & Sons, Inc., 2012.

Smith, Bud E. *Facebook for Business in 10 Minutes.* USA: Pearson Education, Inc., 2011.

Stephenson, James and Courtney Thurman. *The Ultimate Small Business Marketing Guide.* Irvine, CA: Entrepreneur Press, 2007.

Stephenson, James with Rich Mintzer. *Home-Based Business Handbook.* Canada: Entrepreneur Media, Inc., 2008.

Sutton, Garrett. *The ABCs of Writing Business Plans: How to Prepare a Business Plan that Others Will Want to Read and Invest In.* New York: Business Plus (Warner Business Books), 2005.

Veer, E.A. Vander. *Facebook.* 2nd edition. Sebastopol, CA: O'Reilly Media, Inc., 2009.

Walker, June. *Self-Employed Tax Solutions.* 2nd edition. Guilford, CT: Globe Pequot Press, 2009.

Weiss, Alan, PhD. *Million Dollar Consulting.* 4th edition. Hoboken, NJ: John Wiley & Sons, Inc., 2009

Weiss, Alan, PhD. *The Consulting Bible.* Hoboken, NJ: John Wiley & Sons, Inc., 2011.

White, Sarah. *Marketing.* 2nd edition. New York: Alpha, Inc., 2003.

Wuovo, Jeffrey J. *Retirement Planning.* New York: Alpha Books (published by Penguin Group), 2007.

CONTRIBUTORS

Frank G. Duggan spent thirty years in the United States Marine Corps, having served as an enlisted man and Commissioned Officer. Of his thirty years active duty service, fourteen were spent overseas in various positions and under different circumstances (some much more enjoyable than others). After he retired from the military, he pursued jobs in the private sector. As Vice President, International Business Director of a publishing company, Frank did not enjoy the cloistered and constrained environment inside a start-up area. He discovered he was neither trained for nor emotionally inclined to effectively perform in an organization where people and personality issues, systems shortfalls, and procedural deficiencies all worked against one another. This eye opener gave Frank the perspective that being an independent management consultant might well be the direction he would pursue. And he did.

Mary C. English works as an independent consultant catering to a wide variety of clients. Her current focus is on instructional design, video and multimedia production. Mary has had more than twenty years of experience in designing and producing educational and informational materials for technology. She is currently working on multiple freelance consulting assignments for government agencies, non-profit organizations, and private companies. She has an MA in Educational Technology from George Mason University in Fairfax, Virginia.

Suzanne M. Long has more than thirty-five years' experience as an instructional designer, performance improvement specialist, and educator. Suzanne is an independent consultant serving a wide range of business industries, including public utilities, Fortune 500 companies, healthcare, and hospitality organizations. Her current focus is on designing training and work process performance interventions for all levels of employees within government, corporate, and small business arenas. She has an MA in Human Resource Development from Marymount University in Arlington, Virginia.

Meryl Rowley (PMP) has worked for the last twenty years in the fields of adult learning, business operations and performance improvement. She runs her own consulting firm and has experience managing and developing customized project management and performance solutions for clients in diverse markets; including government and industry. Ms. Rowley is a highly regarded instructor in the field of Project Management and currently teaches for ESI International (George Washington University), Northern Virginia Community Collage, and Northeastern University. She worked for Xerox Corporation where she served in a variety of positions in operations and training. She instructed employees in Total Quality Management (TQM) methodologies and application projects, helping Xerox to receive the coveted Malcolm Baldridge National Quality Award. She also participated in Xerox' business development of Quality Partnerships with the U.S. Departments of Veterans Affairs and Commerce in Washington, D.C. While a project manager, Ms. Rowley managed program development in project management, sales training, and multimedia/online learning programs. She has held several director-level positions in Organizational Development and Learning in the D.C. Metro areas. Ms. Rowley holds an M.A. in Human Performance Systems from Marymount University, a Training Specialist Certificate from Georgetown University, and a Master's Certificate in Project Management from the George Washington University. She is a certified Project Management Professional, Six Sigma Green Belt and a certified e-learning instructor on Blackboard, where she has developed project management training programs. Ms. Rowley owns her own consulting firm, *Journey Beyond, Inc.*

Laurence E. Rudolph has more than twenty years' experience as a researcher and consultant. He held a research faculty position at Virginia Tech. He was a principal investigator on projects for the US Departments of Commerce and Labor, Nation Institutes of Science, and NIMH. He spent ten years as a senior analyst for Xerox at their National Training Center and was a delegate to an international task force on ISO standards for telecommunications. For the past six years he has run his own consulting firm with clients from the Fortune 100. He earned a BA in Economics from the University of Maryland, an MA in Psychology from Western Michigan University (WMU) and a Doctorate in Research and Evaluation from the Evaluation Center at WMU. Laurence owns his own consulting company, Rudolph Associates, Inc.

ABOUT THE AUTHOR

Leticia (Letty) Gallares Japzon currently works as an independent management consultant specializing in instructional systems design and technical writing and editing, and offers services to private and public organizations.

She is the author of *Succeeding in America: Lessons from Immigrants Who Achieved the American Dream* and *Consulting Today* and has written dozens of articles on business and education.

Letty has lived in the Washington, D.C. area since 1971. She has an MA in Education and Human Development from George Washington University and an MA in Human Resource Management from Marymount University.

Index

Books from Allworth Press

Allworth Press is an imprint of Skyhorse Publishing, Inc. Selected titles are listed below.

Infectious: How to Connect Deeply and Unleash the Energetic Leader Within
by Achim Nowak (5 ½ x 8 ¼, 232 pages, hardcover, $24.95)

Power Speaking: The Art of the Exceptional Public Speaker
by Achim Nowak (6 x 9, 256 pages, paperback, $19.95)

Pocket Small Business Owner's Guide to Building Your Business
by Kevin Devine (5 ¼ x 8 ¼, 256 pages, paperback, $14.95)

The Pocket Small Business Owner's Guide to Business Plans
by Brian Hill and Dee Power (5 ¼ x 8 ¼, 224 pages, paperback, $14.95)

The Pocket Small Business Owner's Guide to Negotiating
by Kevin Devine (5 ½ x 8 ¼, 224 pages, paperback, $14.95)

The Pocket Small Business Owner's Guide to Taxes
by Brian Germer (5 ¼ x 8 ¼, 240 pages, paperback, $14.95)

Brand Thinking and Other Noble Pursuits
by Debbie Millman (6 x 9, 336 pages, hardcover, $29.95)

Emotional Branding, Updated and Revised Edition: The New Paradigm for Connecting Brands to People
by Marc Globe (6 x 9, 352 pages, paperback, $19.95)

Design Thinking: Integrating Innovation, Customer Experience, and Brand Value
by Thomas Lockwood (6 x 9, 256 pages, paperback, $24.95)

The Art of Digital Branding, Revised Edition
by Ian Cocoran (6 x 9, 272 pages, paperback, $23.95)

The Pocket Legal Companion to Trademark: A User-Friendly Handbook on Avoiding Lawsuits and Protecting Your Trademarks
by Lee Wilson (5 x 7½, 320 pages, paperback, $16.95)

The Pocket Legal Companion to Copyright: A User-Friendly Handbook for Profiting from Copyrights
by Lee Wilson (5 x 7½, 320 pages, paperback, $16.95)

Turn Your Idea or Invention into Millions
by Don Kracke (6 x 9, 224 pages, paperback, $18.95)

The Entrepreneurial Age
by Larry C. Farrell (6 ¼ x 9 ¼, 352 pages, paperback, $27.50)

Smart Consumer's Guide to Building Good Credit: How to Earn Good Credit in a Bad Economy
by John Ulzheimer (5 ¼ x 8 ¼, 216 pages, paperback, $14.95)

Legal Forms for Everyone, Fifth Edition
by Carl W. Battle (8 ½ x 11, 240 pages, paperback, $24.95)

To see our complete catalog or to order online, please visit *www.allworth.com*.